Marginality of Visible Minorities in Canada: A Missiological Study

Nestor Abdon & Enoch Wan

Diaspora Series of CDRR

Marginality of Visible Minorities in Canada: A Missiological Study

Copyright 2023 © Western Academic Publishers

Nestor Abdon & Enoch Wan

Cover designed by Mark Benec

ISBN: 978-1-954692-19-0

All rights reserved. Except for brief quotations in critical publications or reviews, no part of this book may be reproduced in any manner without prior written permission from the publisher or author.

CDRR (Center of Diaspora & Relational Research) @ https://www.westernseminary.edu/outreach/center-diaspora-relational-research

TABLE OF CONTENTS

LIST OF TABLES vii
LIST OF FIGURES ix
FOREWORD xi
CHAPTER 1 INTRODUCTION 1
    Introduction 1
    Background of this Book 2
    Background of the Co-Authors 3
    The Purpose of this Book 4
    The Readership of this Book 5
    Definition of Key Terms 6
    The Organization of the Book 8
CHAPTER 2 BACKGROUND UNDERSTANDING OF THE TOPIC 11
    Introduction 11
    Thematic Background 11
    Theoretical Background 12
    Methodological Background 15
    Summary 16
CHAPTER 3 INTERDISCIPLINARY AND INTEGRATIVE VIEW OF MARGINALITY: AN OVERVIEW OF THE CONCEPT 17
    Introduction 17
    Marginality in Sociology 18
    Marginality in Economics 21
    Marginality in Psychology 24
    Marginality in Anthropology 25
    Integrative View of Marginality 28
    Summary 31
CHAPTER 4 MISSIOLOGICAL PERSPECTIVE OF DIASPORA MARGINALITY: BIBLICAL, SCRIPTURAL, AND THEOLOGICAL FOUNDATIONS 33
    Introduction 33
    Biblical Perspective 33
    Scriptural Foundation 37
    Theological Perspective 45
    Summary 49

CHAPTER 5 NATURE OF ETHNICITY: ITS ROLE IN MARGINALITY AND ITS MISSIOLOGICAL PURPOSE 51
Introduction 51
The Meaning of *Ethnos* 51
Ethnic Inequality in the Bible 54
Missiology of Ethnicity: Biblical and Scriptural Perspectives 55
A Theology of Ethnicity 62
Summary 65

CHAPTER 6 ETHNICITY AND NATURE OF MARGINALITY OF DIASPORA VISIBLE MINORITIES IN CANADA 67
Introduction 67
A Review of Concepts 67
Ethnic Composition of Diaspora Visible Minorities in Canada 73
History of Marginality of Diaspora Visible Minorities in Canada 78
Nature of Marginality of Diaspora Visible Minorities in Canada 84
Summary 92

CHAPTER 7 MISSIOLOGICAL UNDERSTANDING OF MARGINALITY: TOWARDS THE DEVELOPMENT OF RELATIONAL MARGINALITY FOR LEADERSHIP DEVELOPMENT 95
Introduction 95
Transformational Models of Marginality 95
Relational Marginality 101
Conceptual Framework 102
Missiological Implications of Relational Marginality 106
Leadership Development of Diaspora Visible Minorities: From Marginality to Relational Marginality 110
Leading from Marginality to Relational Marginality 118
Summary 120

CHAPTER 8 SUMMARY, CONCLUSIONS, AND RECOMMENDATIONS 123
Introduction 123
Summary of Findings 123
Conclusion 129
Recommendations 130

APPENDIX 1 RESEARCH DESIGN AND METHODOLOGY 133
Methodological Design 133

Research Procedures and Techniques 134
Collection of Data 135
BIBLIOGRAPHY **137**

LIST OF TABLES

Table 1. Old Testament Biblical Foundation of Migration and Marginality 41

Table 2. New Testament Biblical Foundation of Migration and Marginality 42

Table 3. Scriptural Foundation of Migration and Marginality 43

Table 4. Continuation of Scriptural Foundation of Migration and Marginality .. 44

Table 5. Population of Visible Minorities 75

Table 6. Canada Visible Minorities Labour Force Participation, Employment Rate, Unemployment Rate 2021 86

Table 7. Pre-COVID-19 Job Loss, COVID-19 Impact on Financial Obligations, and Income Support Among Visible Minorities 87

LIST OF FIGURES

Figure 1. In-Between (classical self-negating definition of marginality) 97

Figure 2. In-Both (self-affirming definition of marginality) 98

Figure 3. In-Beyond (holistic definition of marginality) 99

Figure 4. Creator and Creature in Relation to Each Other 104

Figure 5. Relational Marginality in the Context of Hermeneutical Community 112

Figure 6. Leadership Development in a Relational Framework 116

Figure 7. Leading from Marginality to Relational Marginality 119

Figure 8. Phases of Transformational Change 120

FOREWORD

In many ways, it would be easier for me to write in general terms about the 272 million people who live as migrants today. There is something strangely safe to talk about migration from the safe distance of "millions." It seems cleaner, softer perhaps to talk about how those millions of people have made decisions to leave their homeland, their family, their language. They decided to leave the patterns of life that they had known because there was something in that new land that was somehow to be preferred.

It likewise seems cleaner and softer to note that, accompanying migration, we see the ugliness and pain of marginalization. "You are not from here, are you?" is the common thread that ties those hundreds of millions together. What gave them away? Was it their clothing? Their accent? The color of their skin? Their preferences in food or in family patterns? What does it mean to be the "outsider?"

Given the audience of this book, most of us will see migration and marginalization through the eyes of missiology – through the eyes of God's mission to bring redemption, grace, healing and restoration. We will be aware of the statistics and the global trends that push/pull people from one nation to another. We will look at the overarching trends of how many households speak multiple languages, and how many households are multigenerational. We will be aware of the trends and we will know how those trends tie into social and theological topics.

If you are like me as I read this book the first two times, even as a missiologist you will read from the safe distance of "millions."

But for Pauline, it is not a topic that is safely distanced from everyday reality. Her native West Africa gave her a strong faith in Christ and strong bonds with family. Her love for her family brought her across the ocean and, more importantly, across life patterns. But she found that the "pull" of economic advancement came at the cost of being "the other" – set aside as different because of her food, her speech, her forms of worship (even though still Christian), her surname, her ways of raising a family. Her ways of expressing thoughts and of relating to the people around her all made it clear that "she is not from here."

I can't think about Pauline from the safe distance of "one of 272 million." Pauline lives in my neighborhood. Her experiences, like those that you will see in Enoch Wan and Nestor Abdon's book, are very real. They are not so clean nor safe. She has so much to offer her new home, and she could be so well served by that new home... and yet the relational divisions and barriers keep her separate. Marginalized. "Other."

I could tell the same story about Roberto and his family from Eastern Cuba and their experiences as newcomers to life in New Jersey, United States. So much hope and courage, and so many opportunities and yet so quickly dismissed as simply "the other."

My hope is that all of us mission-minded readers will come to this book with three perspectives. The first of those perspectives is that "softer, cleaner" big picture (massively big picture) of millions of displaced refugees and other migrant populations. Keep that big picture in mind. Mission is indeed about multitudes. Studying what God is doing in and through "every tribe and tongue and nation and people" calls us to see statistics and trends and chronologies. The big picture matters.

The second perspective I urge us to keep in mind is our own community. The flesh and blood people, families, adults and teenagers and children and grandparents who live near you. I didn't use real names, but Roberto and Pauline are both real people. You probably don't know the individuals I am thinking of, but you know many others like them. Whether you live in Europe or Latin America or North America or Australia or Asia.... missiology is not a distant reality. It lives just down the street from you, and from me.

There is a third perspective for all of us too. In the beautiful words of Colombian poet and singer, Santiago Benavides[1]:

Dios también fue inmigrante
Dios también tuvo que huir
Dios también fue desplazado y estuvo deprimido y sin ganas de seguir
Dios también perdió a su niño
Dios también probó la soledad
Dios también se quedó sin amigos cuando más precisaba su solidaridad
Dios también, Dios también, Dios también pasó por el dolor.
Dios también, Dios también. Dios también lloró.

Permit me to translate, with apologies that this translation shares none of the beautiful feel that is found in Benavides' poem:

God as well was an immigrant
God as well was forced to flee
God as well was a "displaced person", depressed, not wanting to go on.
God as well lost His Son.
God as well tasted loneliness

---

[1] Santiago Benevides, Dios Tambien. Reorded on "Un Lugar Llamado Gracia"

God as well was left without friends when He most needed their solidarity.
God as well, God as well, God as well went through pain.
God as well, God as well, God as well wept.

That third perspective? As Nestor Abdon and Enoch Wan's book will unfold for you – when we think of the issues of migration and marginalization, we find ourselves thinking of millions of people. And we find ourselves thinking of that individual person from halfway around the world who crossed the street with you this morning. We also think of the Creator of all humanity who lived as a stranger on the land He created. This topic brings us into the missiology of kindness, of bridge-building, of reconciliation. It brings us to the missiology of a redemption that breaks down the barriers and replaces them with relationships that cross from person to person, and from person to God. It brings us a missiology that says we ourselves are "the other" living in this world but not of this world, awaiting the day when we are in our own homeland.

Dr. Mark R. Hedinger
Director: CultureBound
Adjunct: Western Seminary, Portland, OR

CHAPTER 1

INTRODUCTION

Introduction

Marginality is often understood and explained in the context of social conflict. This is particularly true with regards to racial or ethnic identities as the location or dislocation of racialized groups are always understood as the product of discrimination and racism. The movement of people through migration further exacerbates the conflict as host societies or the majority culture in a host country sense that the influx of other ethnicities will change their cultural and social fabric. Host societies and majority cultures also consider themselves as having the central location in society and immigrants are seen as foreigners or "the other." Cullen and Pretes suggest that "demonizing of the foreign and strange is probably a universal practice, and marginality is likewise a universal construct. Every society defines itself as central, with the foreigners and strangers lying outside deemed marginal."[2] A theological and missiological understanding of marginality, however, enables us to move beyond the framework of social conflict or seeing only the inherent negativities of human suffering and move into the valuing of human experience as central to God's redemptive work. This is not to abrogate the hardships and suffering experienced by immigrants or diaspora peoples as they move into a new country. Injustice, discrimination, and racialization are not conditions to be passively acquiesced to as God calls his people to seek justice and compassion to foreigners (Lev. 19: 34; Matt. 25: 35-40). This is to underscore the importance of a theocentric worldview where the center of all reality is God. Thus, migration and the consequent marginality are central to God's revelation and redemptive purpose for the nations.

In viewing marginality from a theocentric perspective, marginality is more than a matter of social dislocation but stems from our broken relationship with God and redounds to broken relationships within humanity. The missiological purpose of this study of marginality in the context of diaspora peoples is then apropos to the overarching divine plan rather than a circumstantial product of social dynamics. It is not a problem to be solved but a condition that needs to be understood within such divine purpose.

---

[2] Bradley T. Cullen and Michael Pretes, "The Meaning of Marginality: Interpretations and Perceptions in Social Science," *The Social Science Journal* 37, no. 2 (2000): 216.

The focus of this book is to delve into the biblical, scriptural, and theological foundations of the missiological purpose of diaspora marginality with the hope that it will be a resource in equipping Christian diaspora communities into avenues for active mission work in their new home and develop pathways for mission leadership. It is the hope of the authors that a practical application of this missiological understanding will contribute to their leadership development in mission.

Background of this Book

While migration is part of human history, the movement of peoples in the 21st century is unprecedented. The current migration estimate puts the number of international migrants to 272 million.[3] Of these, 25.9 million are refugees and 41.3 million are internally displaced people due to violence and conflict.[4] Migration shapes human behaviour as people adapt to environmental, social, and cultural changes. With the move into a new place, there are broad areas of adjustment that migrants need to contend with.

A significant adjustment of immigrants is the process of trying to integrate into the new social and cultural fabric of the host community or country. While migration presents possibilities for a better life, this is not a benign experience devoid of any relational dynamics between the diaspora and host communities. The reality of living in a new social, cultural, and geographic milieu is affected by power structures that make integration a challenge.

In the Canadian context, immigrants or diaspora communities who are of non-European background and who are officially termed as visible minorities by the Canadian government, significantly experience economic, political, and social dislocation.[5] Diaspora marginality is therefore directly tied to ethnic or racial identities. In subscribing to the issue of marginality, particularly as an issue of power relations of being in the fringes of the social and cultural milieu of the host community or country, the researchers sought to highlight the condition of immigrants as a perpetual experience of powerlessness that affect their sense of belonging and identity. In most cases, the immigrants' journey is not met by hospitality of the host community.

---

[3] Marie McAuliffe, Binod Khadria, and Céline Bauloz, eds., *World Migration Report 2020* (Geneva: International Organization for Migration, 2019), 3.

[4] McAuliffe, et al., eds., *World Migration Report*, 3.

[5] As defined by Statistics Canada, visible minorities are "persons, other than Aboriginal peoples, who are non-Caucasian in race or non-white in colour." The visible minority population consists mainly of South Asian, Chinese, Black, Filipino, Latin American, Arab, Southeast Asian, West Asian, Korean, and Japanese. In, Statistics Canada, "Visible Minority of Person," https://www23.statcan.gc.ca/imdb/p3Var.pl?Function=DEC&Id=45152.

Marginality based on ethnicity or race is of significant concern as this negates God's creative act of ethnic diversity and his purpose of proclaiming his name to the nations. Yet it is in this condition of powerlessness and marginality that God reveals his redemptive purpose. The book attempts to reclaim and renew focus on Jesus' juxtaposition of Kingdom values of marginality with that of the values and structures of the world that seek premium on power and centrality (Matt. 20: 20-28). For Jesus, the actuality of the Kingdom on earth necessitates a shift from the world's preoccupation with centrality towards valuing those in a state of marginality and situating the realization of the Kingdom in the place of marginality.

The book seeks to establish the definitive role of marginality in God's redemptive message and how this message is embedded in the lived marginal experience of immigrants. While migration is central to God's revelation and redemptive purpose to the nations, there is a dearth of studies on the relationship between marginality and mission. This book seeks to contribute to the field of diaspora missiology by focusing on one critical diaspora experience and condition that is to be understood as essential to God's missional purpose to the nations.

Background of the Co-Authors

Nestor Abdon is a missiologist who seeks to understand the nature of diaspora movements in the context of God's redemptive purpose. This is reflected in his ministry experience at Knox Presbyterian Church as local and global missions Pastor where he seeks to lead the church in equipping and strengthening its hospitality posture and celebration of diversity. He also served at The Peoples Church as Newcomers Ministry Pastor, where he developed the hospitality ministry for newcomers to Canada. In this responsibility, he elevated the role of churches in the newcomer settlement process by spearheading program collaboration with non-profit settlement organizations. He also worked with refugees at Adam House Refugee Centre that enabled him to catalyze churches to support refugee housing. His current ministry focus is co-facilitating the establishment of Diaspora Ministry Coalition that enables Visible Minority diaspora Christian leaders to share mission models. Nestor holds a degree in Doctor of Public Administration from the University of the Philippines-Diliman and Doctor of Intercultural Studies from Western Seminary in Portland, Oregon. He also holds a Certificate in International Development Management Studies from Humber International Development Institute and Certificate in Refugee Studies from York University.

Enoch Wan has served on the faculty at Western Seminary for twenty-three years, leading three doctoral programs in intercultural studies and intercultural education. He served for two terms as president of the Evangelical Missiological Society and as vice president in various capacities for two decades. Enoch began his research on the two paradigms (i.e., relational realism and diaspora missiology) during his sabbatical as scholar-in-residence at Yale Divinity School two decades ago. Since then, he has published many articles and dozens of books on these two themes.[6]

The Purpose of this Book

Immigrants or diaspora peoples face a plethora of challenges in leaving their places of origin and move into a new geographic, social, and cultural milieu. A study by Bhugra and Becker revealed that cultural bereavement is one of the main factors affecting migrants.[7] They stated that, "migration involves the loss of the familiar including language (especially colloquial and dialect), attitudes, social structures, and support network."[8] Thus, migration results in deficit of relationships that originally provides anchor to one's sense of belongingness and identity.

The background of the study also revealed deficiency of relationships between immigrants and host communities or countries. The state of marginality of immigrants is a failure of hospitality and uneven power relations. Averil Bell stated that "hospitality encompasses a complex and power-laden set of relations between people and places."[9] In this regard, Wieland stated that:

> It is the host who holds power, assumes ownership of the place of meeting, sets the conditions on which the guest might enter and be welcomed, and any subsequent relationship might proceed, and controls the mode of relating. The structure of such a relationship impedes its development towards fuller mutuality and the emergence of a new reality.[10]

Such a deficit of relationship between diaspora and host communities is contrary to the scriptural injunction of welcoming the strangers and treat them like native-born (Lev. 19: 33-34). This failure further adds credence to the

---

[6] See Appendix 2 for a list of publications on the relational paradigm and the diaspora missiology paradigm.

[7] Dinesh Bhugra and Matthew A. Becker, "Migration, Cultural Bereavement and Cultural Identity," *World Psychiatry* 4, no. 1 (February 2005): 18–24, https://www.ncbi.nlm.nih.gov/pmc/articles/PMC1414713/.

[8] Bhugra and Becker, "Migration, Cultural Bereavement and Cultural Identity," 19.

[9] Avril Bell, "Being 'at Home' in the Nation: Hospitality and Sovereignty in Talk about Immigration," *Ethnicities* 10, no. 2 (May 27, 2010): 240, https://doi.org/10.1177/1468796810361653.

[10] George M. Wieland, "Finding Communitas in Liminality: Invitations from the Margins in the New Testament and in Contemporary Mission," in *We Are Pilgrims: Mission From, In and With the Margins of Our Diverse World*, ed. Darren Cronshaw and Rosemary Dewerse (Dandenong: UNOH, 2015), 75.

missiological call to humanity to be in relationship with God, for to be in positive relationship with God can transform human relational dynamics.

There is also a deficiency of relationships between host churches and immigrant church communities. Diaspora mission seems to be focused on mission to diaspora communities. Considering migrants as the target of mission upholds the power-laden relationship between host churches and diaspora communities. The leadership skills of the diaspora communities are lost in what could be a strong mission partnership. This relational dynamic is expressed in the tendencies of multiethnic churches to still be led by leaders of majority culture. Both immigrant churches and legacy churches also have tendencies to be culturally homogeneous due to lack of engagement, with most immigrant churches existing in silos.

The book looks at the essential cause of marginality, and that is the relationship deficit between the creator God and humanity due to sin, which caused relationship breakdown among people. These perverted relationships result in power dynamics and ethnic marginality. The study of diaspora marginality provides significant theological and missiological understanding of an adverse experience by delineating its purposive nature. It also underscores the role of immigrants as messengers of God's message of redemption and reconciliation through their lived experience.

As the issue of marginality has been delineated from a relational perspective, the Relational Interactionism framework will be the analytical tool to be utilized. In utilizing this framework, it is the purpose of the book to highlight the causality, dynamics, and consequences of relationships in understanding reality.

The Readership of this Book

It is assumed that since this book is a missiological study, it has value only among diaspora missiologists and cross-cultural practitioners who are serving people on the move and those doing mission among diaspora communities. This book intends to see these people avail of its value:

- Christian visible minorities in Canada who seek to understand their experience and condition.
- Racialized communities or visible minorities who are in the process of seeking the ways of Jesus.
- Congregants who seek to welcome immigrants into their spaces of worship and ministry.
- Pastors of multiethnic churches.
- Church boards seeking to promote staff diversity and address power dynamics in intercultural teams.

- Leaders of Christian visible minority communities who are exploring their role in church and mission leadership.

Definition of Key Terms

Archival Research- Archival research is a design that uses and analyzes existing data. Of particular interest in this research is the use of literature review and secondary data analysis.[11]

Biblical- This refers to narratives or literature that are found in the Bible without any reference to a specific injunction or command. These are not universal or prescriptive in nature and are usually context-specific.

Diaspora- Diaspora is the dispersion or scattering of people from their places of origin.[12]

Diaspora Missiology- Diaspora missiology is "a missiological framework for understanding and participating in God's redemptive mission among people living outside their place of origin."[13]

Diaspora Marginality- The state of diaspora visible minorities being on the fringes of host societies resulting in powerlessness and non-recognition of their cultural values and ethnic identities. To be marginal also means being a cultural outsider.[14]

Integrative Research- Integrative research is a research approach that is designed to be "theoretically coherent, thematically consistent, methodologically complimentary and structurally unified."[15]

Marginality- From an economic perspective, marginality refers to being in the periphery of primary resources. Sociologically, it refers to being in the fringes of primary groups.[16] Anthropologically, it pertains to an individual's or community's racial, socio-economic status, and ethnic identities that provide socio-cultural positions within a specific society that results to discrimination and inequality. Theologically, marginality is the product of transgressional

---

[11] W. Paul Vogt, Dianne C. Gardner, and Lynne M. Haefelle, *When to Use What Research Design* (New York: Guilford Press, 2012), 86.

[12] "Diaspora," *Oxford Reference*, https://www.oxfordreference.com/view/10.1093/oi/authority.20110803095716263.

[13] Lausanne Movement, "The Seoul Declaration on Diaspora Missiology," November 14, 2009, https://www.lausanne.org/content/statement/the-seoul-declaration-on-diaspora-missiology.

[14] Mary Yoko Brannen, Stacey R. Fitzsimmons, and Yih-teen Lee, "Marginals as Global Leaders: Why They Might Just Excel!" *The European Business Review* (n.d.), https://www.academia.edu/2417702/Marginals_as_Global_Leaders_Why_they_might_just_excel.

[15] Enoch Wan, "Inter-Disciplinary and Integrative Missiological Research: The 'What,' 'Why,' and 'How'," *Global Missiology* 4, no. 14 (July 2017): 2.

[16] Cullen and Pretes, "The Meaning of Marginality," 217.

change brought primarily by destruction of relationship the Triune God and humanity and resulting in unequal relations among people groups. Missiologically, it is an embodiment of servanthood and recognition of the centrality of and reliance on God.[17]

Migration- Migration refers to the movement of peoples from their places of origin to a new place either temporarily or permanently.[18]

Missiology- Generally, it means the study of missions. Descriptively, it means establishing a framework in understanding and participating in the mission of God (*missio Dei*) using scriptural, theological, and social science tools.

Missiological Implications- Conclusion of a missiological nature drawn from the study of God's redemptive purpose of historical events. In this regard, these are not explicitly stated but understood by the researcher as implicit meanings that have bearing on mission.

Relational Interactionism- Relational Interactionism is an interdisciplinary framework developed from practical considerations of interaction of personal Beings/beings forming realistic relational network, in multiple contexts, and with various consequences."[19]

Relational Transformation- A transformation brought about by the relationship of the individual with the Triune God. This in turn results in transformation in the individual's relationship with others (horizontal relationship). Transformation occurs through the process of being, belonging and becoming.[20]

Scriptural- This denotes universal and prescriptive message of God in any generation and context.[21] Scriptural injunctions are universal and are "binding for people at all times."[22]

Social Marginality- This perspective holds that power is the central determinant of marginality, with a group considering itself as the center and viewing minorities and nonmembers as marginal.[23]

STARS- *STARS* is a criterion in ensuring that research is doctrinally sound, evangelical, and theologically grounded. The acronym stands for scripturally

---

[17] A substantive treatment of the subject is discussed in Chapter 3 of this book.
[18] *Cambridge Advanced Learner's Dictionary & Thesaurus*, https://dictionary.cambridge.org/dictionary/english/migration.
[19] Enoch Wan and Jon Raibley, *Transformational Change in Christian Ministry*, 2nd Ed. (Portland, OR: Western Academic Publishers, 2022), 9.
[20] Enoch Wan, "Narrative Framework for Relational Transformational Change," 2021, 9.
[21] Wan, "Inter-Disciplinary and Integrative Missiological Research," 6.
[22] Wan, "Inter-Disciplinary and Integrative Missiological Research."
[23] Cullen and Pretes, "The Meaning of Marginality," 217.

sound, theologically supported, analytically coherent, relevantly contextual, and strategically practical.[24]

Theologizing- Theologizing is the act of developing a theological argument and treating a topic from a theological point of view. In this case, the topic of marginality in the context of the immigrants' experience.

Theology- Theology is the understanding of our 'knowledge of God.[25] In this book, it refers to the understanding of God and his purpose relative to the immigrants' state of marginality in his overall design of revealing himself and his act of redemption.

Transformational Change- The "dynamism and process of positive change, originating vertically from the Triune God and ushered in the relational reality horizontally, through the process of interaction between personal Beings (the Triune God) and human beings, at micro and macro (personal and institutional) levels and multiple dimensions (i.e., spiritual, moral, social, and behavioral)."[26]

Transgressional Change- Change caused by the enemy of the Triune God and are thereby "contrary to the attributes of God and his will."[27]

Visible Minority- These are "persons, other than Aboriginal peoples, who are non-Caucasian in race or non-white in colour."[28] The visible minority population consists mainly of South Asian, Chinese, Black, Filipino, Latin American, Arab, Southeast Asian, West Asian, Korean, and Japanese.[29]

The Organization of the Book

The book is organized into eight chapters.

Chapter 1 provides the background and purpose of the book.

Chapter 2 presents key literature and research pertinent to the study objectives. This literature review includes materials related to thematic focus on diaspora mission, the theoretical literature on immigrant marginality, and methodological literature on the use of archival research.

Chapter 3 provides an overview of the meaning of marginality from different disciplines such as Sociology, Economics, Psychology, and Anthropology. From these different disciplines, an integrative understanding of marginality is delineated in the context of the scriptural view of marginality as a result of relational breakdown between the Creator and humanity.

---

[24] Wan, "Inter-Disciplinary and Integrative Missiological Research," 6-7.

[25] See, Erik Thoennes, "What Is Theology?", *The Good Book Blog - Talbot School of Theology Faculty Blog*, May 16, 2016, https://www.biola.edu/blogs/good-book-blog/2016/what-is-theology.

[26] Enoch Wan, "Relational Transformational Leadership: An Asian Christian Perspective," *Asian Missions Advance*, April 2021, 2–7.

[27] Wan and Raibley, *Transformational Change in Christian Ministry*, 7.

[28] Statistics Canada, "Visible Minority of Person,"

[29] Statistics Canada, "Visible Minority of Person."

Chapter 4 provides an analysis of biblical, scriptural, and theological foundations of the missiological understanding of diaspora marginality. Based on the interdisciplinary delineation of marginality in the previous chapter, it is then integrated into the broader framework of God's redemptive purpose. In this chapter, the idea of a transformed view marginality is proffered. In this regard, the state of marginality of immigrants is understood in the context of God's mission.

Chapter 5 is a biblical, scriptural, and theological exploration of ethnicity and how this is foundational to diaspora marginality. The movement of different ethnic groups across geographic boundaries creates ethnic divisions. Diaspora marginality is first and foremost an issue of ethnic or racial inequality.

Chapter 6 presents the ethnic composition of visible minorities in Canada and their experience of marginality. This also provides clarity of the terminologies used, particularly the concept of visible minority as a differentiator of ethnic groups experiencing such marginality. This also delineates the limits of the term due to current concerns on racism and racial discrimination.

Chapter 7 explores the conceptual and theological framework of Relational Marginality, determines its missiological purpose, and applies it in the context of diaspora visible minorities as agents of God's redemptive purpose.

Chapter 8 presents the summary, conclusion, and recommendations derived from the study of diaspora marginality. It presents research concerns that were not covered by the book and could be further explored as new research directions.

CHAPTER 2

BACKGROUND UNDERSTANDING OF THE TOPIC

Introduction

The exploration of thematic, theoretical, and methodological background in this chapter is to ground the study on other literature and research that are pertinent to the marginality of diaspora visible minorities. While there will be an exhaustive and comprehensive treatment of the topic and relevant areas in other chapters, this background is foundational as a general framework for understanding the theme of migration, the theoretical foundations of missiological understanding of marginality, and appropriate exploration of integrative research approach and archival methodology to come up with appropriate missiological findings.

Thematic Background

Migration is not a new phenomenon. Historical and biblical stories reveal the movement of people. The current movement of people through migration and displacement is unprecedented this 21st century. The world is seeing tremendous human movement and human suffering due to ethnic conflicts, wars, and poverty. Cities are changing due to the movement of people from rural to urban areas. People from two-thirds world are also moving to western countries in search of a better future. Climate change is bringing out new forms of refugees. The office of the United Nations High Commissioner for Refugees (UNHCR) reports that there are currently more than 79.5 million people who are forcibly displaced, and of these, 26 million are refugees.[30]

While historical realities present this movement of people as consequence of wars, poverty, and the need for economic opportunity, this is not incidental to God's salvation history and the *missio Dei*. One concrete example is the movement of Israel as a diaspora community and as a nation chosen by God for his mission. Christopher Wright categorically defined the role of Israel (and the whole testimony of the Old Testament), as being chosen to be a blessing for the nations.[31] What was established with Israel was a missional covenant. In the same manner, Jesus' mission and that of the Church, is the ingathering of

---

[30] United Nations High Commissioner for Refugees, "Figures at a Glance," June 18, 2020, https://www.unhcr.org/figures-at-a-glance.html.

[31] Christopher J.H. Wright, *The Mission of God: Unlocking the Bible's Grand Narrative* (Downers Grove, Illinois: IVP Academic, 2006), 454-500.

nations.³² Both Jesus and Paul see their mission work as an "eschatological necessity."³³ In this manner, the mission to the nations or every cultural, racial, and language group ("*panta ta ethne*") necessitates a cross-cultural endeavor.³⁴ The Pentecost affirmed that diaspora is a key mission platform by enabling the disciples to speak in different languages, thus becoming a model to "communicate the Good News of the mighty Acts of God in Christ, to every people in their heart language and culture."³⁵

This statement is, however, more than a call for cross-cultural missions. Implicit in this is the reality that people are on the move and God fulfills his mission in this movement. In this regard, the movement of peoples is not just the impact of sin but a way for God to spread his message of salvation to the nations. The Lausanne movement recognized this movement of God among the people in diaspora by affirming diaspora missiology as "a missiological framework for understanding and participating in God's redemptive mission among people living outside their place of origin."³⁶ In this missiological framework, diaspora mission becomes a strategic initiative of reaching migrants with the gospel. Yet the second component of diaspora missiology is the affirmation that diaspora communities themselves are agents of God's mission. Wan and Tira, in their study on the Filipino diaspora experience, stated that "in recent decades, it has become common knowledge among missiologists that there are mission initiatives from the diaspora Christian communities."³⁷

The focus of diaspora missiology is keenly relevant and important in the context of Canada. There is a significant shift in the social and religious climate of the country due to immigration that has clear missiological implications.

Theoretical Background

Migration is a disorienting experience of seeking to make sense of the new reality. Some scholars tend to view this as a state of liminality or what Victor Turner called an in-between state of a person or community that has left one

---

³² Wright, *The Mission of God*, 501-530.

³³ Wright, *The Mission of God*, 511.

³⁴ Paul Pierson E., *The Dynamics of Christian Mission: History Through a Missiological Perspective* (Pasadena, CA: WCIU Press, 2009), 19.

³⁵ Pierson, *The Dynamics of Christian Mission*, 23.

³⁶ Lausanne Movement, "The Seoul Declaration on Diaspora Missiology," November 14, 2009, https://www.lausanne.org/content/statement/the-seoul-declaration-on-diaspora-missiology.

³⁷ Sadiri Joy Tira and Enoch Wan, "The Filipino Experience in Diaspora Missions: A Case Study of Christian Communities in Contemporary Contexts," *Evangelical Missiological Society*, (April 5, 2008): 3. http://www.wcc2006.info/fileadmin/files/edinburgh2010/files/Study_Process/EDINBURGH%20COMMISSION%20VII%20tira%20diaspora.pdf.

condition but has not integrated into the new one.[38] Wieland added that "liminality is characterized by disorientation, discomfort and a destabilizing of the settled order. It is accordingly rich in potential for new orderings of experience and understanding, the emergence of new relationships and ways of being, indeed for transformation."[39]

While the migration experience presents possibilities, this is not a benign experience devoid of any relational dynamics between diaspora and host communities. In Sang Hyun Lee's study of the Asian American experience, he considered this condition as forced liminality and even defined marginality in this way. He states that:

> Their liminality exists in the context of nonacceptance by the dominant group. Their liminality is made permanent by the barrier of the dominant group's nonacceptance. In such a situation, the creativity of liminality cannot flourish, nor can any fruits of the in-between experience be brought back productively into a structure. Such liminality, then, is a frustrated and suppressed liminality, and the people caught in it are deprived of completing the process of human becoming. By the term marginality, then, we mean a forced and permanent liminality—an in-betweenness that is suppressed, frustrated, and unfulfilled by barriers that are not in one's control.[40]

The reality of living in a new social, cultural, and geographic milieu is affected by power structures that make integration not only a challenge but also just an aspiration. It could be a constant and perpetual struggle for parity for immigrants. Thus, the experience and state of marginality is a reality that constrained integration in the new environment.

In subscribing to the issue of marginality, particularly as an issue of power relations of being in the fringes of the social and cultural milieu of the host country, the study sought to highlight the condition of immigrants as more than a state of liminality or in an 'in-between state' but a real and perpetual experience of powerlessness and being in the margins that affect their sense of belonging and identity.

---

[38] Victor Turner, "Liminality and Communitas," in *The Ritual Process: Structure and Anti-Structure* (Chicago: Aldine Publishing, 1969), 94–113, 125–30.

[39] Wieland, "Finding Communitas in Liminality," 71.

[40] Sang Hyun Lee, "Pilgrimage and Home in the Wilderness of Marginality: Symbols and Context in Asian American Theology," in *Korean Americans and Their Religions: Pilgrims and Missionaries from a Different Shore*, eds. Ho Youn Kwon, Kwang Chung Kim, and R. Stephen Warner (Pennsylvania: Pennsylvania State University Press, 2001), 58–59.

Transformational Change Paradigm

The process of immigrants' making sense and adjustment to marginality is reflective of the transformative learning theory that focuses on adult learning process or andragogy. In delineating transformative learning theory, Jack Mezirow alluded to the human need to navigate and assess contested meanings to arrive at interpretations of beliefs and life assumptions that are true or justifiable through critical assessment of these assumptions made by self and others.[41] Thus, he defined transformative learning as "the process of using prior interpretation to construe a new and revised interpretation of the meaning of one's experience as a guide for future action."[42]

An adult can make a critical reflection on one's and other's assumptions to come up with a choice of true or justified belief by being involved in critical discourse as this involves a critical assessment of assumptions. Ultimately, the contribution of transformative learning is that it leads an individual to reflectively process his or her beliefs, values, and mindsets to determine a course of action that leads to becoming "liberated, socially responsible, and autonomous learners."[43] But this is only possible if there is a supportive relationship and supportive environment that would foster this learning process.[44]

In the Christian context, Wan argued that transformation occurs through the individual's relationship with the Triune God (vertical relationship) and with fellow Christians (horizontal relationship).[45] From this perspective, transformative change does not just take place through 'critical discourse' as Mezirow claimed but through a relationship with the Triune God and the relational community.[46]

The state of marginality of diaspora individuals and communities calls for a transformative change. This necessitates understanding their current state of marginality to create a new meaning of such marginality. From a Christian context, their relationship with God and his household (*oikos*) creates a new meaning of their foreigner status (*paroikos*) and state of marginality as a condition of value and dignity. It is a new condition that is not dictated by those in the center but in their new understanding of such marginality as a location in

---

[41] Jack Mezirow, "Learning to Think Like an Adult: Core Concepts of Transformative Theory," in *Learning as Transformation: Critical Perspectives on a Theory in Progress* (San Francisco, CA: Josey-Bass, 2000.), 3–4.

[42] Mezirow, "Learning to Think Like an Adult," 5.

[43] Mezirow, "Learning to Think Like an Adult," 30.

[44] Mezirow. "Learning to Think Like an Adult," 25.

[45] Enoch Wan and Mark Hedinger, "Transformative Ministry for the Majority World Context: Applying Relational Approaches," *Occasional Bulletin*, Spring 2018, 8.

[46] Wan and Hedinger, "Transformative Ministry for the Majority World Context," 8.

the Kingdom (Matt. 20: 20-28). Relationship is also key to the leadership development of diaspora leaders.

The study delineated the practical application of the learning points through strategic recommendations that give bearing on missiological models for diaspora Christian leaders and host churches in utilizing a transformed view of marginality as a missiological outcome.

Methodological Background

The book made use of an interdisciplinary understanding of diaspora marginality by looking into the understanding of this reality from different disciplines such as sociology, economics, anthropology, and psychology. These perspectives were then grounded on the scriptural view of marginality because of the breakdown of humanity's relationship with the Triune God. This then resulted in negative relational dynamics that distorted power relations where diaspora visible minorities were forced into the margins of social, economic, and cultural fabric of host societies.

Understanding immigrant marginality as an essential part of God's mission to the nations requires in-depth analysis of biblical and scriptural foundations and other literature and research that have bearing on the subject. Thus, the study made use of archival research. Archival research is the use of secondary data to cull information not only on biblical and scriptural foundations but on contemporary phenomenon of migration and marginality. Archival research also serves to determine theological foundations that reflect on the issue. The delineation of this research approach subscribes to its general meaning of the use of literature review and secondary data analysis in coming up with conclusions on the research objectives. The study contextualized the issue of immigrants' marginality in the situation of visible minority immigrants in Canada. This then explored missiological implications and determined practical application in mission training related to relational marginality utilizing the relational transformation lens.

The STARS approach[47] guided the methodological process starting with scriptural exploration to ground the study on God's missiological purpose. The study sought to attain analytical coherence through review and analysis of relevant research and theories and by grounding the findings on scripture and sound theology. In this regard, the issue of diaspora marginality in terms of multiple disciplines such as economics, sociology, anthropology, psychology and others is interpreted within the framework of humanity's marginality or separation from the Trinitarian God as revealed in scripture. Thus, marginality is the product of man's rebellion and separation from his creator, and concomitantly resulting in humanity's separation from each other.

---

[47] Wan, "Inter-Disciplinary and Integrative Missiological Research," 6–7.

The contextual nature of the book is through analysis of the state of marginality from the immigrants' experience. Of import is the situation and experience of Canadian evangelical Christian immigrants in church and mission participation.

The book delineates the practical application of the learning points through strategic recommendations that give bearing to the leadership development of Christian diaspora leaders in church formation and mission participation. In this regard, leadership development of Christian diaspora leaders is directed towards relational leadership where the relational pattern within the Triune God is expressed as the model for their reconciliatory and mission work.

The delineation of the missiological purpose of diaspora marginality and the consequent leadership development of Christian diaspora leaders are grounded on the integrative methodology that sought to define marginality beyond the notion of social, economic, or cultural marginalization but as a direct result of the relational dynamics between the Triune God and his creation.

Summary

The delineation of thematic, theorical, and methodological background provided relevant studies and literature that bear significance on the theme and focus of the study of diaspora marginality. The literature further gave credence to what research and writings have been done so far regarding diaspora marginality and how this book adds to the existing body of knowledge. An exhaustive treatment of interdisciplinary and integrative understanding of marginality in the next chapter leads readers into deeper theoretical and thematic exploration of the concept.

CHAPTER 3

INTERDISCIPLINARY AND INTEGRATIVE VIEW OF MARGINALITY:
AN OVERVIEW OF THE CONCEPT

Introduction

The concept of marginality is complex with varied perspectives and subjectivities. There is a general idea, however, that marginality is defined and delineated as the process of confining or relegating individuals or communities to a lower or inferior status, or of less importance. In this regard, marginality could be spatial, where people are situated in specific spaces, or social, where there is an experience of powerlessness due to their ethnicity, gender, economic status, etc.

How does one categorize a people or community as marginal? In the context of diaspora peoples, this could be determined by ethnicity, geographic origins, or social position in the host country. Yet the very nature of migration is already a condition of marginality. The universality of marginal treatment and condition of immigrants is valid in all of history; so much that the Bible anchored the story of salvation in the context of the experience and journey of immigrants (1 Peter 2: 11-25). Furthermore, scriptural injunctions on the way that God's people are commanded to compassionately treat the foreigners only affirm the universality of this marginal treatment (Lev. 19: 9-10; Lev. 19: 15; Deut. 15: 7-8; Matt. 25: 31-46). God emphasizes the marginal status of foreigners by locating them in the same position as the widows, orphans, and the poor. The Israelites were also instructed to treat foreigners as they would the poor (Lev. 15: 35). Of interest is that "laws benefiting the poor were common in the ancient Near East, but only the regulations of Israel extended this treatment to the resident foreigner."[48] Thus, the focus of immigrant or diaspora marginality is central to the calling for a different way of relationship for God's people.

It is, therefore, imperative to provide a clear definition and delineation of marginality from different disciplines to come up with a sound epistemological foundation. The idea of diaspora marginality is therefore not an assumption about the objective reality of diaspora experience but needs to be understood

---

[48] TOW Project, "Gleaning (Leviticus 19: 9-10)," https://www.theologyofwork.org/old-testament/leviticus-and-work/holiness-leviticus-1727/gleaning-leviticus-19910.

in the context of these variety of perspectives. In a way, it could not just be assumed that all diaspora peoples and communities are marginal or are in a state of marginality. Interestingly, the term marginality was first introduced by Robert Park as a scientific concept in the context of migration particularly in the late 20th century.[49] For Park, migration results to a different form of behavior for a person who is living in two diverse cultures—a marginal man.[50] "It is in the mind of the marginal man that the conflicting cultures meet and fuse."[51] Park views marginality as a situation of being in-between cultures and is not able to integrate due to racial prejudice. Despite racial prejudice, he still proffers that progress is basically a product of migration and such progress is substantially created by this marginal man. Thus, he claims, "it is in the mind of the marginal man that the moral turmoil which new cultural contacts occasion manifests itself in the most obvious forms. It is in the mind of the marginal man—where the changes and fusions of culture are going on—that we can best study the processes of civilization and of progress."[52]

The value of delineating an interdisciplinary and integrative understanding of marginality further sheds light not only in a clear understanding of the nature of marginality but on how these connect with diaspora experience. Fields such as economics, anthropology, and other social science disciplines provide critical analysis of marginality and thereby provide manifold lenses on the concept. The integrative understanding explains marginality from a broader theocentric framework.

Marginality in Sociology

A social construct is something that exists due to human interaction. Sociologists Peter Berger and Thomas Luckmann originally argued that society is created by human interaction.[53] Any reality is to be, therefore, explained by studying such interaction and the underlying causes, consequences, and context of such interaction.

Robert Park introduced marginality as a sociological concept. His idea of marginality, however, is more of cultural ambivalence, or of a person living in-between cultures.[54] It was Stonequist, however, who gave further elaboration

---

[49] Alexey Borisovich Lebedev et al., "Marginality in the Socio-Philosophical and Juridical Dimensions: The Experience of an Interdisciplinary Approach," *Revista San Gregorio*, no. 34 (November 2019): 10.

[50] Robert E. Park, "Human Migration and the Marginal Man," *American Journal of Sociology* 33, no. 6 (1928): 881.

[51] Park, "Human Migration and the Marginal Man," 881.

[52] Park, "Human Migration and the Marginal Man," 893.

[53] Peter L. Berger and Thomas Luckmann, *The Social Construction of Reality: A Treatise in the Sociology of Knowledge* (London: Penguin Books, 1966).

[54] Park, "Human Migration and the Marginal Man."

on Park's concept in his iteration of The Marginal Man. In his conception, the marginal man is an individual who moves from one culture to another but not belonging to either.[55] In reflecting on the contribution of Park in the development of the concept in sociology in a sixty year period, Billson was able to determine three forms of the concept: Cultural marginality refers to delineating people according to race, ethnicity, religion, and other cultural differences, and putting valuation based on these characteristics; Social role marginality occurs "when an individual cannot fully belong to a positive reference group because of age, timing, situational constraints, or when an occupational role is defined as marginal" and; Structural marginality, which "refers to the political, social, and economic powerlessness of certain disenfranchised and/or disadvantaged segments within societies. It springs from location in the socioeconomic structure of society, rather than from cultural or social role dilemmas."[56]

From Weisberger's perspective, Park's delineation of marginality is unidirectional where it leads to fusion of cultures. Thus, Weisberger categorically states:

> His image of being betwixt and between is unidirectional, whereas the marginal person is caught in a cross-current, located within a structure of double ambivalence. This person is ambivalent toward his or her own culture, wants to return but cannot, wants to leave but cannot do that either; and is ambivalent toward the new culture, wants to assimilate but cannot, and wants to reject it but cannot.[57]

While still delineating marginality in the context of immigrants, Weisberger further alludes to the complexity experienced by immigrants that has clear bearing on other people who are socially excluded. He states that "being a stranger, a wanderer confronting an alien if not hostile culture, lies at the heart of marginality. Marginality implicitly refers to a condition of cultural inequality, which may, but need not, interact with political and economic inequality."[58]

As an issue of exclusion, marginality was given substance by Emile Durkheim through his concept of alienation. Durkheim coined the term "anomie" or normlessness which refers to "the breakdown of social bonds between an individual and his community ties, resulting in the fragmentation of

---

[55] Everett V. Stonequist, *The Marginal Man: A Study in Personality and Culture Conflict* (New York: Charles Scribner's Sons, 1937).

[56] Janet M. Billson, "No Owner of Soil: The Concept of Marginality Revisited on Its Sixtieth Birthday," *International Review of Modern Sociology* 18 (Autumn 1988): 183–204.

[57] Adam Weisberger, "Marginality and Its Directions," *Sociological Forum* 7, no. 3 (1992): 429.

[58] Weisberger, "Marginality and Its Directions," 431.

social identity."[59] Durkheim put forward a thesis that one of the purposes of social order is social solidarity and this is reinforced by social values including its religion and moral values. Alienation as predicated on the breakdown of social or community ties is substantially studied by Durkheim in his seminal work on suicide.

In his analysis of Durkheim's work, Shepard stated that "some aspects of social behavior—even something as allegedly individualistic as suicide—can be explained without reference to the individual."[60] He referenced one type as anomic suicide, Shepard revealed that these empirical research findings on suicide are purely secondary to his main concern. First, behavior can be explained by social rather than psychological factors. And second, behavior is affected by the degree of social integration and regulation.[61] A key aspect in this reflection is that marginality as alienation is the result of being separate from social ties. This is a condition experienced by those who are considered not part of the mainstream or dominant group in society.

While Durkheim's premise is grounded on the reality of the 19th century industrialization where social relationships are impacted by specialization of labor, it is still a cogent way of analyzing the impact of social distancing in the present climate brought about by the influx of immigrants in a host country and the resulting ethnic divisions, gentrification in urban communities, wealth inequality, and other forms of social divisions. Among the excluded, their sense of social identity is removed. Interestingly, the concept of anomie is even applied in the context of the pandemic where social distancing became the norm. In this regard, the new norm of social distancing has removed the collective bond.[62]

A clearer definition of marginality as social exclusion is categorically defined in the Social Construction model as delineated by Cullen and Pretes.[63] This perspective holds that socio-political power is the central determinant of marginality, with a group considering itself as the center and viewing minorities and non-members as marginal.[64] While the study of Cullen and Pretes tried to determine how scholars in the social sciences in the U.S. and

---

[59] "Alienation," *Social Science LibreTexts*, August 22, 2018, https://socialsci.libretexts.org/Bookshelves/Sociology/Introduction_to_Sociology/Book%3A_Sociology_(Boundless)/17%3A_Population_and_Urbanization/17.04%3A_Urban_Life/17.4F%3A_Alienation.

[60] Jon Shepard, *Sociology*, 10th ed. (California: Wadsworth Publishing Company, 2009), 50.

[61] Shepard, *Sociology*, 50.

[62] Massey Howes Ellie, "Durkheim's Anomie in a Time of Crisis," July 9, 2020, https://liberalarts.org.uk/durkheims-anomie-in-a-time-of-crisis/.

[63] Cullen and Pretes, "The Meaning of Marginality," 215-229.

[64] Cullen and Pretes, "The Meaning of Marginality," 217.

Canada define marginality, it helped in identifying two definitions of marginality as either from an economic standpoint or those who consider it as a social construction. In particular, the study provides clarity of social exclusion by studying "the underlying reasons for exclusion, inequality, social injustice, and the spatial segregation of people."[65] In stating marginality as social exclusion, it is important to delineate the reference point that identifies who are in the center and who are in the margins. Gatzweiler et al. correctly point this out: "Marginality can only be properly defined in a specific reference context. In social systems, marginalized people are often defined as subgroups that differ from the core or mainstream. The core group in this respect is the reference group that the outlier subgroups are marginal to."[66]
Marginality as a social construct provides a definition that delineates power dynamics and spatial position of an individual or community in a social or cultural context.

Marginality in Economics

A significant use of marginality as a conceptual framework is in the field of economics and economic development, particularly in examinations of poverty and development of peoples and regions. Interestingly, a study by Gatzweiler and Baumüller that tries to examine the multi-dimensionality of poverty made use of marginality as a multi-disciplinary framework in understanding the former. Thus, in using marginality as a multi-disciplinary framework, they made use of the definition by Gatzweiler, Baumüller, Ladenburger, and von Braun as:

> An involuntary position and condition of an individual or group at the margins of social, political, economic, ecological and biophysical systems, preventing them from access to resources, assets, services, restraining freedom of choice, preventing the development of capabilities, and eventually causing extreme poverty.[67]

While it might be correct to assume that marginality in this context can be characterized from a multi-disciplinary approach and that poverty is multi-

---

[65] Franz W. Gatzweiler and Heike Baumüller, "Marginality—A Framework for Analyzing Causal Complexities of Poverty," in *Marginality: Addressing the Nexus of Poverty, Exclusion and Ecology*, ed. Joachim von Braun and Franz W. Gatzweiler (Dordrecht: Springer Netherlands, 2014), 31.

[66] Franz W. Gatzweiler, et al., "Marginality from a Socio-Ecological Perspective," in *Marginality: Addressing the Nexus of Poverty, Exclusion and Ecology*, ed. Franz W. Gatzweiler and Joachim von Braun (Dordrecht: Springer Netherlands, 2014), 57.

[67] Franz W. Gatzweiler et al., "Marginality: Addressing the Root Causes of Extreme Poverty," *ZEF Working Paper Series 77* (Center for Development Research, University of Bonn, 2011), 3.

dimensional, there is a pervading theme of marginality as a matter of the degree of access to resources.

While this book is not a study on poverty, the economic or development perspective on marginality provides another dimension to the concept. It is important to note as well that in the context of diaspora studies, it is not only social and cultural exclusion that diaspora peoples are experiencing in a host country but also limited access to resources due to barriers put in place that prevents such access. This is predominantly true in the Canadian context particularly in economic and labor opportunities.

As an economic construct, marginality could also be traced to the concept of alienation. A categorical view in this regard is Karl Marx's theory of alienation. Originally a philosophical treatise which later became categorically a critique of Capitalism, Marx argued that "labor is central to a human being's self-conception and sense of well-being."[68] In a way, work provides a worker with a sense of identity through what he produces. As Capitalism is the system of the private ownership of the means of production (land, capital, machineries, factories, etc.), this deprives the workers of "this essential source of self-worth and identity."[69] It is to be understood, however, that alienation is not just a matter of subjective or emotional reaction to being separated from the means of production that provides such self of worth and identity. For Horowitz:

> Alienation is not meant by Marx to indicate merely an attitude, a subjective feeling of being without control. Although alienation may be felt and even understood, fled from and even resisted, it is not simply as a subjective condition that Marx is interested in it. Alienation is the objective structure of experience and activity in capitalist society.[70]

Alienation in this regard is about an experience of being excluded from control over resources and production process. Marginality as alienation from access to and control of resources has gained significant scholarship. The study of Cullen and Pretes on the perspectives on marginality among scholars in the US and Canada revealed that aside from being understood as social construction, many define it as an economic concept. In this regard, economic determinants define marginality. The economic perspective views marginality as a condition of regions that are distant from the markets.[71] Their economic conception of marginality is not on marginality in general but as an issue of

---

[68] Sparknotes, "Karl Marx (1818–1883): Themes, Arguments, and Ideas," *SparkNotes*, https://www.sparknotes.com/philosophy/marx/themes/.
[69] Sparknotes, "Marx."
[70] Asher Horowitz, "Marx's Theory of Alienation" (Lecture, Department of Political Science, Faculty of Liberal Arts and Professional Studies, York University, 2012), https://www.yorku.ca/horowitz/courses/lectures/35_marx_alienation.html.
[71] Cullen and Pretes, "The Meaning of Marginality," 217.

marginal regions, particularly utilizing the center or core/periphery model.[72] This perspective is generally defined by the World Systems model of the sociologist Immanuel Wallerstein which is a legacy of Marx's social theory.[73] While Marx viewed marginality as a lack of control over resources in a capitalist society, Wallerstein applied it in the broader inter-regional or transnational capitalist arrangement of labor.[74] Elwell succinctly expressed Wallerstein's meaning of the core/periphery:

> The capitalist world-system is based on a two-fold division of labor in which different classes and status groups are given differential access to resources within nation states; and the different nation states are given differential access to goods and services on the world market. Both types of markets, those within and those between nation states, are very much distorted by power…. The peripheral areas are the least developed; they are exploited by the core for their cheap labor, raw materials, and agricultural production. The semi-peripheral areas are somewhat intermediate, being both exploited by the core and take some role in the exploitation of the peripheral areas.[75]

In reflecting on the model in the context of migration, it could be construed that migration is a product of this transnational movement of labor where highly skilled migrants are both syphoned by core (western) regions for their skillset and at the same time compels migrants to seek better economic opportunities in core regions due to low wages in peripheral countries as a result of exploitation by these core regions. The "brain drain" phenomenon or human capital flight has been extensively studied and documented. An early study by the International Monetary Fund revealed the extent of brain drain from developing countries to the US and OECD countries, which shows that in the Asia Pacific region, the biggest source of highly skilled labor is the

---

[72] Cullen and Pretes, "The Meaning of Marginality," 217.

[73] An earlier work on World Systems theory is Andre Gunder Frank's concept of "Development of Underdevelopment" or dependency theory which states that underdevelopment of poor countries is not due to structural issues within the country but a product of exploitation by core countries. See, Andre Gunder Frank, "Development of Underdevelopment," *Monthly Review* 41, no. 2 (June 1989).

[74] See Immanuel Wallerstein's four-volume reinterpretation of global history, *The Modern World System*. In this four-volume study of World Systems, he traces the Capitalist growth from the 16th century Mercantilist movement to the 20th century's triumph of Liberalism as the dominant ideology.

[75] Frank W. Elwell, "Wallerstein's World-Systems Theory," http://www.faculty.rsu.edu/users/f/felwell/www/Theorists/Essays/Wallerstein1.htm . For a comprehensive treatment, see, Frank W. Elwell, *Macro-Social Theory*, 2nd ed. (CreateSpace Independent Publishing Platform, 2015).

Philippines.[76] The study further revealed that investments in education could not offset this brain drain unless there are higher incentives to stay. Thus, the study of marginality from an economic perspective is not just an exercise in militancy but a genuine concern for the plight of developing and poor countries that are the main source of migration. On an individual level, this becomes a concern for the plight of migrants who experience economic marginality in host (core) countries.

Marginality in Psychology

A psychological understanding of marginality is often situated in the context of migrants. Their experience is usually delineated as that of alienation and loss. A study by Bhugra and Becker revealed that cultural bereavement is the main factor that affects migrants.[77] In a way, "migration involves the loss of the familiar including language (especially colloquial and dialect), attitudes, social structures, and support network."[78] Another view focuses on the issue of identity. In the context of migration, Mahalingam posits that "studies of immigrant identity, in particular, face unique challenges because immigrants need to cope with dual worldviews and negotiate multiple identity demands as a consequence of their displacement."[79]

This sense of alienation of migrants should go beyond their experience of displacement, however, and on the overall state of marginality as social and political exclusion. From this perspective, other groups in society that are marginalized also experience oppression and discrimination. There are significant psychological impacts of this experience as this affects the mental health of people in a state of marginality. Hudick suggests that "both physical and social separation from society can contribute to a dissonance in connection to community."[80] Another psychological impact of marginality is the sense of inferiority. Thus, Granger concedes that "one of the most difficult feelings to rid oneself of is the emotional turmoil associated with being marginalized by a

---

[76] William J. Carrington and Enrica Detragiache, "How Extensive Is the Brain Drain?," *Finance and Development: A Quarterly Magazine of the IMF* 36, no. 2 (June 1999), https://www.imf.org/external/pubs/ft/fandd/1999/06/carringt.htm.

[77] Dinesh Bhugra and Matthew A. Becker, "Migration, Cultural Bereavement and Cultural Identity," *World Psychiatry* 4, no. 1 (February 2005): 18–24, https://www.ncbi.nlm.nih.gov/pmc/articles/PMC1414713/.

[78] Bhugra and Becker, "Migration, Cultural Bereavement and Cultural Identity," 19.

[79] Ramaswami Mahalingam, "Power, Social Marginality, and the Cultural Psychology of Identities at the Cultural Contact Zones," *Human Development* 51, no. 5–6 (2008): 368.

[80] Katie Hudick, "Community Psychology's Impact on Public Health and the Experience of Marginalization," *Community Psychology*, n.d., 9.

person or group in the position of power. Feelings of anger and confusion are often followed with those of inferiority."[81]

It is clear that a common denominator in the discussion of marginality in the field is in terms Social Psychology. While individual expressions and effects are given prominence, it is always explored in a social context. Thus, the lack of opportunity for social contribution leads to low self-esteem and the lack of ability to participate in community life leads to further isolation.[82] In-depth studies on the relationship between mental health and marginality have identified social determinants of such mental health concern. One classic example is that done by Anglin et al., that suggests inequitable social and economic system in society significantly influences psychotic risks.[83]
Other psychological studies and perspectives on marginality focus on the positive aspects in shaping identity that is in the same vein of that of Hook's view of marginality as site of resistance where it offers new possibilities.[84] Wilson also seeks to study further this positive nuance of marginality as it relates to experience of shaping everyday life.[85]
In analyzing research on the psychological perspective on marginality, the focus has been on social determinants of mental health rather than the meaning of marginality itself. In this regard, the experience of marginality leads to mental health issues.

Marginality in Anthropology

An anthropological view of marginality focuses on the issues of race, socio-economic status, and ethnic identities as providing socio-cultural positions within a specific society that results in discrimination and inequality. As Cultural Anthropology is "the description, interpretation, and analysis of similarities and differences in human cultures,"[86] it provides a distinct way of

---

[81] Nathaniel Granger, "Marginalization: The Pendulum Swings Both Ways," *Unbound* (blog), April 5, 2013, https://www.saybrook.edu/unbound/marginalization/.

[82] Mark Burton and Carolyn Kagan, "Community Psychology: Why This Gap in Britain?" (Manchester Learning Disability Partnership and Manchester Metropolitan University, n.d.).

[83] Deidre M. Anglin et al., "From Womb to Neighborhood: A Racial Analysis of Social Determinants of Psychosis in the United States," *American Journal of Psychiatry* 178, no. 7 (July 2021): 599–610.

[84] Bell Hook, *Feminist Theory: From Margin to Center* (Boston: South End Press, 1984).

[85] Janelle Wilson, "Marginality: A Key Concept Revisited," *Psychology Today*, September 14, 2015, https://www.psychologytoday.com/ca/blog/stories-the-self/201509/marginality-key-concept-revisited.

[86] Brian Howell M. and Jenell Paris W., *Introducing Cultural Anthropology: A Christian Perspective* (Michigan: Baker Academic, 2011), 4.

viewing marginality. From this perspective, marginality or inequality in societies is constructed through the creation of social structures or social organization. Social structure "refers to the ways people coordinate their lives in relation to one another at the level of society."[87]

A result of society's ways of organizing itself is arranging this structure according to wealth, power, and prestige. These three areas are used for social stratification or the organization of people according to hierarchy or rank within a society. By this very nature, social stratification results in social inequality or the "differential access to economic resources, political power, and social prestige."[88] In urban settings, differentiation in gender, ethnicity, educational level, and other social and cultural distinctions is used not only for social stratification but utilized to further limit access to economic resources and power. For many, this could lead to spatial marginality. This is evidenced by either ghettoization or rise of slum communities.

A common tool for social stratification is race. Race is "a cultural category that divides the human race into subspecies based on supposed biological differences."[89] Race is a social construct rather than biological differentiation. While it is true that there are biological differences in people, most of these are given social meaning.[90] Thus, those who control power and resources are by themselves creating differentiation based on supposedly biological characteristics, categorizing others as of lower capacity. The American Anthropological Association categorically corrected this and proffered that the modern racial construct was postulated by European colonialists to justify slavery, colonial conquests, and social stratification and "racial myths bear no relationship to the reality of human capabilities or behavior."[91]

Another anthropological category in analyzing marginality is ethnicity. Ethnicity is based on "group affiliation derived from distinct heritage or worldview as a 'people.'"[92] Essential to this affiliation are cultural features such as language, religion, etc. Biological commonalities could also be used in delineating one's ethnicity. Yet, due to these cultural distinctions, in similar vein as race, this is also used for social stratification and exclusion.

Of particular concern is in the area of migration where ethnicity is part of the cultural construct by host societies of using ethnicity for exclusion, discrimination, and categorization of people from different ethnicities as "the other." In the Canadian context, the migration trend gave rise to an institutional

---

[87] Howell M. and Paris W., *Introducing Cultural Anthropology*, 66.
[88] Howell M. and Paris W., *Introducing Cultural Anthropology*, 66.
[89] Howell M. and Paris W., *Introducing Cultural Anthropology*, 71.
[90] Howell M. and Paris W., *Introducing Cultural Anthropology*, 71.
[91] "AAA Statement on Race," *American Anthropological Association*. https://www.americananthro.org/ConnectWithAAA/Content.aspx?ItemNumber=2583.
[92] Howell M. and Paris W., *Introducing Cultural Anthropology*, 77.

distinction of people who are non-white or non-European descent as visible minorities. Visible minorities are "persons, other than Aboriginal peoples, who are non-Caucasian in race or non-white in color."[93] The visible minority population consists mainly of South Asians, Chinese, Black, Filipino, Latin American, Arab, Southeast Asian, West Asian, Korean, and Japanese.[94] Currently, visible minorities make up 60.2% of first-generation Canadians.[95]

The use of the term 'visible minority,' as applied to these ethnicities, is already an act of marginalization where non-white or non-Caucasian backgrounds are lumped outside of the majority culture and are thereby distinct. This is interchangeably used with the term 'racialized' people or communities or systemic marginalization of certain people groups.[96] This distinction of being a minority also means less influence and power due to such ethnic classification.

Another anthropological perspective on marginality is in the context of cultural adaptation or acculturation. Acculturation is the "process of culture change and adaptation that occurs when individuals with different cultures come into contact."[97] Acculturation is categorized into four types: assimilation, integration, separation, and marginalization.[98] Kankesan provided a clear description of these four types:

> Assimilation results from a rejection of one's ancestral culture and complete acceptance of the majority culture. Separation results from a rejection of the majority culture and an isolated envelopment of one's ancestral culture. Marginalization occurs when one is neither a member of the majority culture nor one's ancestral culture. Integration, or biculturalism, occurs when one is a member of both the majority and ancestral cultures.[99]

---

[93] Statistics Canada, "Visible Minority of Person."

[94] Statistics Canada, "Visible Minority of Person."

[95] Statistics Canada, "Generation Status: Canadian-born Children of Immigrants," https://www12.statcan.gc.ca/nhs-enm/2011/as-sa/99-010-x/99-010-x2011003_2-eng.cfm.

[96] Habiba Zaman, "Racialization and Marginalization of Immigrants: A New Wave of Xenophobia in Canada," *Labour/Le Travail* 66 (Fall 2010): 164.

[97] Margaret A. Gibson, "Immigrant Adaptation and Patterns of Acculturation," *Human Development* 44, no. 1 (2001): 19, https://doi:10.2307/26763493.

[98] Veronica Benet-Martinez and Jana Haritatos, "Bicultural Identity Integration (BII): Components and Psychosocial Antecedents," *Journal of Personality* 73, no. 4 (August 2005): 1015–1050, http://doi.wiley.com/10.1111/j.1467-6494.2005.00337.x.

[99] Tharsni Kankesan, "Understanding Bicultural Identity and Its Impact on the Association between Discrimination and Well-Being" (PhD Dissertation, University of Toronto, 2010): 7. http://hdl.handle.net/1807/26277.

In viewing marginality from the perspective of acculturation, this finds similarity in the concept of liminality or a state of in-betweenness. Interestingly, liminality is mostly applied in the context of migration.

In subscribing to the issue of marginality as an issue of power relations and of being in the fringes of the social and cultural milieu of the host country, I seek to highlight the condition of immigrants as more than a state of liminality or in an 'in-between state' but a real and perpetual experience of powerlessness and being in the margins that affect their sense of belonging and identity.

Integrative View of Marginality

The different views of marginality from key disciplines allow for a broader understanding of how it shapes human behaviour and the human condition from different causes and factors. The social sciences are meaningful tools in understanding the human condition. From this, it allows categorical issues affecting diaspora visible minorities and the reality of their situation.

Central to an integrative definition of marginality is to base it on the broader conception of reality beyond human factors and conditions: that is to say, to understand the condition of diaspora visible minorities beyond humanistic interpretations. An integrative view of marginality requires going beyond humanistic interpretations and understand it from theological and spiritual perspectives which view reality as more than the understanding of the natural world. Paul Hiebert sheds light on this in his conception of the excluded middle. He explains that in many societies, the belief in spirits that impinge on human existence is essential to their conception of reality.[100] He postulated that Western thinking delineates only two levels of reality—Religion and Science. Religion is understood to deal only with issues of faith and everything that is an exception to the natural order while science deals with the empirical and natural order. Thus, Hiebert defines the problem of this dichotomization in this manner:

> The result was the secularization of science and the mystification of religion. Science dealt with the empirical world using mechanistic analogies, leaving religion to handle other-worldly matters, often in terms of organic analogies. Science was based on the certitudes of sense experience, experimentation and proof. Religion was left with faith in visions, dreams and inner feelings. Science sought order in natural laws. Religion was brought in to deal with miracles and exceptions to the natural order, but these decreased as scientific knowledge expanded.[101]

---

[100] Paul G. Hiebert, "The Flaw of the Excluded Middle," *Missiology: An International Review* X, no. 1 (January 1982): 35–37.

[101] Hiebert, "The Flaw of the Excluded Middle," 43.

He further alluded to this Western scientific thinking as a mechanical analogy of reality where everything is subject to impersonal forces or impersonal laws of nature. In contrast, the organic analogy sees "the world in terms of living beings in relationship to one another."[102] He stated that traditional religionists see the world using the organic analogy where diseases are understood as caused by spirits. Christians also have an organic view as "Christians see their relationship to God in organic terms. God is a person and humans relate to him in ways analogous to human relationships."[103]

The problematic idea that he sees among Western missionaries, however, is the lack of understanding and recognition of the spirit world that impinge on the human condition. It is this "excluded middle" that needs to be given attention by missionaries in relating to and sharing the gospel in intercultural missions. He proposes a holistic theology that understands reality on three level where there is not only the recognition of the higher cosmic level and the lower natural history that subscribes to "empirical encounter" and secularism, but the inclusion and affirmation of the middle where human history has a "power encounter" that includes recognition of spirits. In this middle level, "a holistic theology includes a theology of God in human history: in the affairs of nations, of peoples and of individuals. This must include a theology of divine guidance, provision and healing; of ancestors, spirits and invisible powers of this world; and of suffering, misfortune and death."[104] At the same time, a holistic theology also includes in the bottom level "an awareness of God in natural history—in sustaining the natural order of things."[105]

There are clear missiological implications to Hiebert's perspective. Central to this is to adopt a posture of relationship in understanding reality so that God will not be a separate entity but someone who is organically connected and in relationship with all aspects of reality. This requires on the part of the missionary to avoid such two-tiered worldview that excludes the middle. For Hiebert, "so long as the missionary comes with a two-tier world view with God confined to the supernatural, and the natural world operating for all practical purposes according to autonomous scientific laws, Christianity will continue to be a secularizing force in the world. Only as God is brought back into the middle of our scientific understanding of nature will we stem the tide of Western secularism."[106]

The implication for explaining the marginality of diaspora visible minorities is significant and clear. Marginality is not just an experience and condition that is caused or influenced by socio-economic factors but on realities beyond

---

[102] Hiebert, "The Flaw of the Excluded Middle," 41.
[103] Hiebert, "The Flaw of the Excluded Middle," 41.
[104] Hiebert, "The Flaw of the Excluded Middle," 46.
[105] Hiebert, "The Flaw of the Excluded Middle," 46.
[106] Hiebert, "The Flaw of the Excluded Middle," 46.

human society. This does not negate the socio-economic factors that marginalize diaspora visible minorities. The delineation of marginality from different disciplines shows the reality of actions of power-laden groups in society to discriminate, exclude, and marginalize the powerless and those viewed as foreign and the other. In looking at the three-tiered perspective, it could be then established that evil and forces against God are at work in distorting human relationships, with scripture claiming, "for our struggle is not against flesh and blood, but against the rulers, against the authorities, against the powers of this dark world and against the spiritual forces of evil in the heavenly realms."[107]

Wan reinforced Hiebert's perspective and put forward the understanding of reality through his conception of relational realism. Relational Realism is "the systematic understanding that 'reality is primarily based on the 'vertical relationship' between God and the created world and secondarily 'horizontal relationship' with the created order."[108] Relational Realism is the foundation for Wan's concept of Relational Interactionism. Relational Interactionism is an interdisciplinary framework developed from practical considerations of interaction of personal Beings/beings forming realistic relational network, in multiple contexts, and with various consequences."[109]

Such perspective affirms the reality of the excluded middle and at the same time affirms the presence and relationship of God in the human sphere. In this relationship, God proffers transformational change through his redemptive act in Christ. Yet the reality of the work of principalities and forces against God in the human realm results in transgressional change. Transformational change is the "dynamism and process of positive change, originating vertically from the Triune God and ushered in the relational reality horizontally, through the process of interaction between personal Beings (the Triune God) and human beings, at micro and macro (personal and institutional) levels and multiple dimensions (i.e., spiritual, moral, social, and behavioral),"[110] while transgressional change is the change caused by the enemy of the Triune God and are thereby "contrary to the attributes of God and his will."[111]

Clearly, marginality is a reflection and result of transgressional change. From a Relational Interactionism perspective, marginality can then be transformed into a (divine) positive reality to become part and even central to God's redemptive purpose. Thus, Christ's death on the cross, while a product of human action, became God's redemptive agency.

---

[107] Eph. 6: 12

[108] Enoch Wan and Mark Hedinger, *Relational Missionary Training: Theology, Theory, and Practice* (Skyforest, CA: Urban Loft Publishers, 2017), 34.

[109] Wan and Raibley, *Transformational Change in Christian Ministry*, 9.

[110] Wan, "Relational Transformational Leadership."

[111] Wan and Raibley, *Transformational Change in Christian Ministry*, 7.

The next chapter presents a comprehensive biblical, scriptural, and theological foundations on the missiological nature and purpose of marginality.

Summary

The exploration of the concept of marginality from several disciplines reveals nuances of the concept, with marginality seen as a negative condition of being excluded, alienated, and geographically and economically in the periphery. These nuances provide a rich perspective as it applies to the situation of immigrants where their foreigner status leads to economic disenfranchisement, social and cultural inferiority, and the concomitant mental health impact of being in the periphery. These disciplines provide clarity and delineation of the struggles of immigrants of being displaced from their social and cultural moorings and be in a new physical, cultural, and social environment. Of particular interest are the experiences of visible minority immigrants in Canada where marginality is a lived experience. Marginality should be understood, however, from an integrative perspective by anchoring it from a Relational Interactionism framework which proffers that marginality is a result of transgressional change. Furthermore, the vertical and horizontal relational nature of reality can transform such transgressional change to fulfill God's redemptive purpose.

CHAPTER 4

MISSIOLOGICAL PERSPECTIVE OF DIASPORA MARGINALITY: BIBLICAL, SCRIPTURAL, AND THEOLOGICAL FOUNDATIONS

Introduction

The integrative view of marginality as presented in chapter 3 provides the framework of its understanding beyond human disciplines and opens the possibility of understanding within the broader framework of a theocentric understanding of reality. From this integrative framework, marginality is the result of the breakdown of the vertical relationship between the Triune God and humanity, and in turn results to a breakdown of horizontal relationship between people where such relational dynamics led to power domination and socio-economic disenfranchisement.

Amid humanity's sin and rebellion, God seeks to restore these relationships. In this process of reconciliation, he uses marginality as an avenue for his redemptive purpose. This integrative understanding of marginality is then to be grounded on biblical, scriptural, and theological foundations.

Biblical Perspective

A Christian view of migration paints a story of the movement of people as a response to God's call (e.g., Abraham's call to build a nation in Gen. 12: 1-15) or a movement directed by God to fulfill his mission to make himself known and to redeem humanity (Acts. 17: 26-27). God also expresses his concern for the foreigners and calls his people to show care and compassion and make them part of the community (Num. 35: 15; Deut. 16:14; Deut. 26:11; Deut. 14:28-29; Lev. 23:22; Eze. 47: 22-23; Isa. 61: 5; Matt. 25: 31- 46; Heb. 13: 1-2). These texts then express God's purpose of migration as a vehicle for his message of redemption and for his people to bear witness to his compassionate nature.

The biblical and scriptural foundations of migration and marginality reveal how God weaved both as purposive in his mission to reveal himself and redeem humanity. Central to this is the story of God's people and their experiences of migration and marginality as instructive of his purpose. Both biblical narratives and scriptural injunctions are presented to express this purpose. The biblical narratives reveal how God's people experienced both migration and marginality. While they are context-specific, they express how these stories and experiences are woven into God's salvation history. Scriptural injunctions reveal his expressed purpose of migration and marginality in his mission.

Old Testament

Migration is woven into the fabric of the Bible so much so that Joan Maruskin proclaimed that the Bible is the ultimate immigration handbook as it is "written by, for, and about migrants, immigrants, refugees, and asylum seekers."[112] God built his salvation history through the migration of his people. In this migration journey, it was also directing them in the space of marginality.

Thus, his act of redemption is integrating both migration and marginality as means to attain his purpose. The story of migration in the Bible starts in the book of Genesis and is introduced early in the third chapter, and that is the exile of Adam and Eve from the garden due to their rebellion against God (Gen. 3: 22-24). The same pattern of migration because of sin follows the story of Cain whose rebellious spirit and the murdering of his brother led to his punishment to wander in the face of the earth (Gen. 4: 10-12). Yet, it is from these migration stories that God also revealed his compassionate nature among these earliest migrants, first with his covering of Adam and Eve's nakedness (Gen. 3: 21) and putting a mark on Cain for his protection (Gen. 4: 15). In a way, central to God's intent for migration is also a call for his people to show hospitality and compassion.

It is also through this migration that God formed nations. It became an avenue for the scattering people to populate the earth (Gen. 9: 19) and establish his covenant to love and protect his creation (Gen. 9: 7- 17). Genesis 10 gives an account of how nations were formed through the three sons of Noah.

As it was God's intent for the scattering of peoples to form nations, humanity went in the opposite direction and expressed their sinfulness and rebellion through re-gathering and centralization (Gen. 11: 1-4). Lee claims "we can conceive that the tower of Babel was the symbol of our rebellion against God's original intent, for it was the symbol of centralization."[113] God's concomitant act of confusing their languages was to cement the purposive nature of the scattering (Gen. 11: 5-9).

God's purpose of migration became a revelatory and redemptive act when he called Abraham to migrate and become a father to a nation that will be a light to the nations (Gen. 12-13). As a light to the nations, Leeman defined this as a broad mission of being God imagers to model God's righteousness and justice. This contrasts with the role of the Church as a narrow mission of

---

[112] Joan Maruskin, "The Bible as the Ultimate Immigration Handbook: Written by, for, and about Migrants, Immigrants, Refugees, and Asylum Seekers" (CWS Immigration and Refugee Program, 2006).
[113] Lee, *Marginality*, 110.

disciple-making and going to the nations.[114] Marginality is essential in God's redemptive purpose. It is interesting to note that God had already forewarned Abraham that his descendants will be aliens and slaves in another country (Gen. 15: 13). In calling Abraham and Sarah to migrate, he also called them into a state of marginality. The book of Hebrews delineated this marginality by stating that "by faith Abraham when called to go to a place he would later receive as his inheritance, obeyed and went, even though he did not know where he was going" (Heb. 11: 8). The warning for his descendants to be aliens and slaves was a clear message that being his chosen people was not a call to centrality. It is to convey his mighty acts and power, and for his people to depend on this power.

Such warning was realized through the migration of Joseph and his family to Egypt (Gen. 37-47). This formation of a nation to be a blessing to other nations started with the experience of marginality of Joseph who was sold by his brothers as a slave (Gen. 37: 12-36). The elevation of Joseph (Gen. 41: 37- 39) and the whole of the Israelite nation into a place of centrality was not a permanent place though as God shifted their location to a place of marginality through enslavement that God forewarned Abraham of. Yet, from the place of marginality, God manifested his power to all the nations through his deliverance of Israel. The book of Exodus is the story of the movement of God's people away from forced marginality towards a new marginality—towards freedom that is dependent on God's provision and power. The first act of God in this deliverance was to call a leader from the place of centrality to marginality. Moses, who experienced a central place in Egyptian society, was called out of this place of centrality and served time as an alien (Exo. 2: 11-22) as part of his leadership training that demanded recognition of God's centrality in this act of deliverance (Exo. 3: 1-22). In the forty-year migration journey, God migrated with his people.[115] The migration journey was an experience of marginality where all that was familiar and sources of security were removed. Yet, they were led into a state of dependence on God for daily sustenance and protection (Exo. 16: 1-36).

The establishment of the nation of Israel in the promised land was supposed to continue this dependence on God for provision and leadership. The judges who served this purpose were appointed by God to lead during times of crisis. First Samuel 8, however, marks a significant shift in the history of Israel when they demanded a king (1 Sam. 8:4-5). The qualification of their statement to demand a king to be like other nations manifests the desire for centrality of temporal power and rejecting God's kingship. God's displeasure (1 Sam. 8: 7-8) is axiomatic of his intent to maintain Israel's marginality as a matter not just of

---

[114] Jonathan Leeman, "Soteriological Mission: Focusing in on the Mission of Redemption," in *Four Views on the Church's Mission*, ed. Jason S. Sexton (Grand Rapids, Michigan: Harper Collins Publishers, 2017), 17–45.

[115] Maruskin, "The Bible as the Ultimate Immigration Handbook," 6.

trust but also of putting God as the center of their national life. The displeasure of God was not merely on their demand for a temporal king but their motive and timing.[116] Garris concludes that God intends for a king to lead Israel (Gen. 17:6; Gen. 17:16; Gen. 35:11; Deut. 17:14-20). Their motive, however, was to have a king to judge them, thus rejecting God as their judge and king. Their demand for an earthly king was also a manifestation of impatience rather than of waiting for God's appropriate moment of appointing a right leader.[117] The desire for centrality (i.e., to be like other nations, rejection of God) led ultimately to their exile and diaspora, first of the Northern Kingdom (2 Kings 17: 5-6), and later of the Southern Kingdom (2 Kings 25: 1-21). In that experience of migration and marginality, God directed his people to place him at the center. Deutero-Isaiah (Isa. 40-66) comprises a rich message of hope to the Israelites through divine deliverance if they return to his fold and at the same time a promise of the messiah and the true king (Isa. 7:14; 11: 2-4; 53:4–5; 61: 1). In this promise of deliverance and rebuilding, God made a place for foreigners:

> And foreigners who bind themselves to the LORD to minister to him, to love the name of the LORD, to be his servants, all who keep the Sabbath without desecrating it and who hold fast to my covenant— these I will bring to my holy mountain and give them joy in the house of prayer. Their burnt offerings and sacrifices are accepted on my altar; for my house will be called a house of prayer for all nations (Isa. 56: 6-7).

New Testament

The gospel accounts in the New Testament start with narratives of migration and marginality. The Gospel of John starts from a cosmic dimension of God's migrating to humanity (John 1: 1; 1: 12). The incarnation as God's migration was also an act of marginality with his creation rejecting him.

The Gospel of Luke starts with a historical account of Jesus' birth as an experience of marginality with the family not being able to find a guest room and ended up being born in a manger (Luke 2: 6-7). It is interesting to note as well that Luke made specific mention of John the Baptist, a marginal figure, to introduce the birth of Jesus (Luke 1: 57-66). Matthew narrates the forced migration of Jesus' family to Egypt due to the threat of violence (Matt. 2: 13-14).

Jesus himself affirmed his state of marginality as a hallmark of his life and ministry. Both Matthew and Luke's Gospels record Jesus' status of being homeless (Matt. 8:19–20; Luke 9:57–58) and conveys a message that those who

---

[116] Zachary Garris, "Did God Intend for Israel to have a King? (1 Samuel 8)," *Knowing Scripture*, March 5, 2019, https://knowingscripture.com/articles/did-god-intend-for-israel-to-have-a-king-1-samuel-8.

[117] Garris, "Did God Intend for Israel to have a King?"

wish to follow him will be in such a state of marginality. The state of marginality is central in Jesus' life and teachings as a calling for his followers. In this regard, marginality is not coincidental but essential in following Christ. It is not just a product of discipleship but a calling to put oneself in the margins. Such calling also involves taking care of those in the margins as these are the ones whom the Kingdom is prepared for (Luke 14: 15-24). Jesus ensures that the foreigners are part of those in the margins that need to be cared for and their care is a precondition for a place in the Kingdom (Matt. 25: 31-46).

While there are few direct statements of Jesus regarding immigrants, his acts that seek inclusivity of foreigners are obvious such as his compassion for the Samaritans (John 4: 4-42) and the healing of the daughter of the Syrophoenician woman (Mark 7: 24-30). In both instances, the Gospel books are expressly emphasizing Jesus' embrace of the 'other' or the foreigner. In Jesus' exchange of words with the Syrophoenician woman, he iterated the Jewish pejorative categorization of outsiders or non-Jews as dogs and consequently honoring the faith of the woman to inform the Jews of his embrace, love, and care for the 'other.' Furthermore, Setzer emphasized that the woman is triple marginalized by being a woman, a gentile, and a foreigner.[118]

Scriptural Foundation

As defined earlier that scriptural denotes universal and prescriptive message of God in any generation and context, there are then key scriptural principles that relate to migration and marginality. Several themes are evident.

Marginality as Kingdom Value

Jesus is clear about marginality as being determined by power. He is also clear that his teachings of the Kingdom from a state of marginality. Twice, he had to rectify his disciples' assumption and preoccupation with power. First when James and John's mother asked for a position of centrality in the Kingdom (Matt. 20: 20-28). He again corrected the disciples when, during the Passover celebration, they argued about who is the greatest in the Kingdom (Luke 22: 24-27).

Living a life of marginality is a constant theme in Jesus' life and his experience of death as an act of redemption maintains this leitmotif. Not only was he rejected by his people and condemned to die (Matt. 27:16-26) but the redemptive nature of his death necessitates even the Father to abandon him (Matt. 27:46; Mk. 15:34). Even the religious establishment marginalized him. The writer of Hebrews stressed the marginal nature of his death by further

---

[118] Claudia Setzer, "The Syrophoenician Woman," *Bible Odyssey*, https://www.bibleodyssey.org/people/related-articles/syrophoenician-woman.

emphasizing that he suffered outside the city gate (Heb. 13: 12-13). Situating him outside the gates or the camp gives meaning to the Old Testament practice of throwing and burning the discarded carcass of sacrificed animals outside Israel's camp (Exo. 29: 14). It also shows the symbolic and theological significance of Jesus act as embracing the experience of being rejected or marginalized and enduring the shame (Heb. 12: 2) for man's salvation.

The Role of Migration and Marginality in Redemption

God affirmed migration and marginality as essential to his revelation and redemptive act. The Great Commission (Matt. 28: 16-20) should not be understood as merely a missionary call of intentionally going to the nations. In mentioning the impending persecution of his followers (Mark 13:9-13), Jesus connects this with the proclamation of the gospel to the nations. In this sense, migration, either because of persecution or intentionally moving to other nations, is seen as a vehicle for gospel proclamation. The book of Acts shows the spread of the gospel through exiled Jewish communities. The movement of the Holy Spirit to bring gospel understanding among people from different ethnicities and languages in Acts. 2: 1-41 harkens back to God's purpose in the Babel experience (Gen. 11: 1-9). It also affirms the missiological purpose of this scattering, and it shows God's movement of blessing the nations and bringing the gospel to the gentiles.

Hospitality and Compassion

There is significance to God's act of covering Adam and Eve's nakedness (Gen. 3: 21) and putting a mark on Cain for his protection (Gen. 4: 15). Amid sinfulness, God has never abandoned humanity and his compassion for the people on a journey. While the Israelites were still on a journey of migration, his constant protection followed them (Exo. 13: 21) and his provision sustained their whole journey (Exo. 16: 1-35). God constantly references Israel as aliens and slaves in Egypt and its deliverance is a template for care for foreigners (Lev. 19: 33-34). During this migration journey, God set these laws and commandments for his people as outlined in Numbers, Leviticus, and Deuteronomy. The institution of this legal care and protection to foreigners will then become a hallmark of anyone who is in covenant with God. This is set forth in his commandment to care for foreigners based on Israel's own experience as foreigners in Egypt (Lev. 19: 34; Deut. 24: 5). Spences noted that the Hebrew term used, "ger," is most translated as a sojourner. While there are several English terminologies for sojourner (alien, foreigner, stranger), the term "conveys the basic idea that a person (or group) is residing, either temporarily or permanently, in a community and place that is not primarily their own and is dependent on the "good-will" of that community for their continued existence."[119] Jobling denotes their landlessness as signifying their marginal status.[120] Their landlessness has significant bearing in their state of marginality that is addressed by God through the gleaning law.

God emphasizes the marginal status of foreigners by locating them in the same position as the widows, orphans, and the poor who lack access to the means of production. Thus, the gleaning law was instituted for such access where farmers were instructed to leave some of the produce to be gleaned by the poor, widows, orphans, and foreigners (Lev. 13: 22; Lev. 19: 9-10; Lev. 23: 22). Deuteronomy 24:19-22 expands on this further by applying the principle to other agricultural products and practices. The Israelites were also instructed to treat foreigners as they would the poor (Lev. 15: 35). Priests were even commanded to use the tithe collected to also help the widows, orphans, and foreigners (Deut. 14: 28-29). Of interest is that "laws benefiting the poor were common in the ancient Near East, but only the regulations of Israel extended this treatment to the resident foreigner."[121] The TOW project (Theology of Work project) clarifies that such commandment to include the foreigners enables God's people to be distinct from other surrounding nations and further states that such law is more than an issue of compassion but of justice. "Through gleaning, the poor earned their living the same way as the landowners did, by working the fields with their labors. It was simply a command that everyone had a right to access the means of provision created by God."[122]

The universal injunction for hospitality to foreigners is evident in its continuation in the New Testament with Jesus consistently locating them in the same marginal space as the poor, widows and orphans, and other marginal groups and declaring that helping them is the same as doing it to him and a prerequisite to being included in his Kingdom (Matt. 25: 31-46). It is in the same vein that the writer of Hebrews reminded his audience to help strangers as such action is also an invitation to God (Heb. 13: 2).

Justice

Marginality as a condition of powerlessness suggests the unjust conditions that foreigners, orphans, the poor, and the widows experience in their daily life. Because of this, God commands his people not to withhold justice to these

---

[119] John R. Spencer, "Sojourner," *Oxford Bibliographies*, June 26, 2019, https://www.oxfordbibliographies.com/view/document/obo-9780195393361/obo-9780195393361-0266.xml.

[120] David Jobling, "Sojourner," in *The New Interpreter's Dictionary of the Bible*, ed. Katharine Doob Sakenfeld, vol. 5 (Nashville, TN: Abingdon, 2009), 314–16.

[121] TOW Project, "Gleaning (Leviticus 19: 9-10)," https://www.theologyofwork.org/old-testament/leviticus-and-work/holiness-leviticus-1727/gleaning-leviticus-19910.

[122] TOW Project, "Gleaning."

marginalized groups (Exo. 22: 21-27; Deut. 24: 17; Deut. 27: 19; Mal. 3: 5). His call for justice in Deuteronomy 24: 17 is then followed by his institution of the gleaning law (Deut. 24: 19-21) which is a concrete act of justice by allowing them to have access to the produce of the land.

The place of centrality is often the source of injustice for this is a position of power. Thus, God's call for justice also demands equality to restore this uneven power relation. He then commands not to show partiality (Lev. 19: 15; Deut. 16: 19) and treat everyone with dignity. Keller contends that universal equality is a distinction of biblical justice and is unique in world history.[123] Having created humanity in his image (Gen. 1: 27) means that everyone has value. The previous statement of Jesus' compassion towards the Samaritans and the Syrophoenician woman shows Christ's spirit of inclusivity that specifically includes the foreigners. It is interesting to note that Jesus' parable of the workers in the vineyard (Matt. 20: 1-16) where workers are waiting the whole day for the landowner to hire them is not just a teaching of the equality of God's grace but is, in fact, a lived experience of undocumented immigrants in the U.S. and Canada who desperately need compassion and justice.

Inclusion in Community

The inclusion of foreigners in Israel's festivals and celebrations has been mandated in its law (Deut. 16:14; Deut. 16: 11). This is a continuation of the original intent to treat foreigners as native-born (Lev. 19: 34) and should be part of the life of the community. In affirming this as a universal mandate for God's followers, this is a call to include foreigners and diaspora communities in the celebration of God's greatness. As God revealed to the Israelites that his act of deliverance will be to proclaim his greatness among the nations, foreigners would have known the story of Israel's deliverance and freedom from slavery.

The book of Ruth also tells a story of a foreigner experiencing marginality who was able to benefit from the gleaning laws (Ruth 2) and her redemption by a kinsman-redeemer to be included in the Israelite nation is a foretaste of Christ's act of redemption for his bride, the Church (Eph. 5: 25-27). The ultimate expression of inclusion is God's call to all nations, tribes, and languages to be under his Kingdom (Rev. 7: 9).

---

[123] Keller, "Justice in the Bible."

Table 1. Old Testament Biblical Foundation of Migration and Marginality

Migration	Marginality
Migration as a result of sin - Adam and Eve were driven out of Eden-Gen. 3:22-24 - Cain's punishment to be a wanderer- Gen. 4: 10-12	Marginality as concomitant to migration - Abraham's descendants will be aliens and slaves- Gen. 15: 13
God's purpose of scattering – - Noah's descendants to populate the earth- Gen. 9:19; Genesis 10 Language differentiation for purposive scattering- - Babel event- Gen. 11: 1-9	Marginality as essential to God's calling and leadership formation - Joseph's slavery- Gen. 37: 12-36 - Slavery of Israelites in Egypt- book of Exodus - Moses' exile to experience marginality- Exo. 2: 11-22; Exo. 3: 1-22
Revelatory and redemptive purpose of migration - Abraham commanded to leave the country- Gen. 12, 13 - Formation of Israel in Egypt through Joseph's exile- Gen. 37-47	Marginality as call to dependence on God - God's daily provision to the Israelites- Exo. 16: 1-36 Centrality as act of rebellion - Israel's demand for a king- 1 Sam. 8: 4-5)
God's migration with his people - Israel's migration to be a chosen nation- Book of Exodus Migration/exile as punishment for centrality - Exile of the two kingdoms- 2 Kings 17: 5-6; 2 Kings 25: 1-21	God's call to his centrality - hope for deliverance of Israel- Isa. 40-66 - Promise of a true king- Isa. 14: 11: 2-4; 53: 4-5; 61: 1

Table 2. New Testament Biblical Foundation of Migration and Marginality

Migration	Marginality
God's act of Migration - Word becoming flesh- John 1: 1, 12	God's act of marginality in migration - God migrating and taking on the form of a slave- Phil. 2: 5-8
God's experience of migration - Jesus and family's exile to Egypt- Matt. 2:13-15	Jesus' state of marginality - Jesus born in a manger- Luke 2: 6-7 - Jesus as homeless- Matt. 8: 19-20; Luke 9: 57-58
Jesus' compassion for and inclusion of foreigners - Jesus' compassion for Samaritans- John 4: 4-42 - Jesus' healing of the daughter of Syrophoenician woman- Mark 7: 24-30	- Jesus rejected by his own people- John 1: 11 - Jesus condemned to die a criminal's death- Matt. 27: 16-26 - Jesus abandoned by the Father- Matt. 27: 46; Mark 15: 34 - Jesus suffered outside the city gates- Heb. 13: 12-13 Christians as marginal people in their earthly status as aliens- 1 Pet. 1: 17-21; 2: 11

Table 3. Scriptural Foundation of Migration and Marginality

Theme	Migration	Marginality
Marginality as Kingdom Value	n/a	The Kingdom and Marginality - Jesus' rebuke of disciples' desire for centrality- Matt. 20: 20-28; Luke 22: 24-27; Matt. 16: 24-25
Role of Migration and Marginality in Redemption	Migration and the spread of the gospel - The great commission- Matt. 28: 16-20 Persecution as a cause of migration - Jesus' forewarns persecution and scattering of disciples- Mark 13: 9-13 Spread of the gospel to the nations - Spirit's language gift to disciples- Acts 2: 1-41	Wisdom of world as foolishness to God - Cross as a power to salvation but foolishness to unsaved- I Cor. 1: 17-21
Hospitality and Compassion	God's act of compassion to those in exile - God covering Adam and Eve's nakedness- Gen. 3: 21 - Mark of protection for Cain- Gen. 4: 15 - God's protection during Israel's migration- Exo. 13: 21; 16: 1-35 God's direct commands for hospitality and compassion - love strangers in their midst- Lev. 19: 34; Deut. 24: 5 - Provision to strangers- Deut. 10:17-19; Deut. 14: 19	Grouping of foreigners with those in the margins - Showing compassion to foreigners, widows, orphans- Deut. 10:17-19; Mal. 3:5 - Caring for strangers, widows, and orphans is caring for Jesus- Matt. 25: 35-41 God's people commanded to share to those in need- Rom. 12: 13

Table 4. Continuation of Scriptural Foundation of Migration and Marginality

Theme	Migration	Marginality
Hospitality and Compassion (cont.)	Gleaning laws for strangers and marginalized groups - Deut. 24: 19-21; Deut. 25:19; Lev. 13: 22; Lev. 19: 9-10; Lev. 15: 35 Hospitality to strangers as hospitality to God - Heb. 13: 2	n/a
Justice for Strangers	Commandment to show justice to strangers and marginalized groups- Deut. 24:17; Deut. 27:19; Exo. 22:21-27 Judgment to those doing injustice to aliens and marginalized groups- Mal. 3:5 Not showing partiality to strangers and marginalized groups- Lev. 19: 15; Deut. 16: 19	n/a
Inclusion in Community	Inclusion in Israel's celebrations- Deut. 16: 14; Deut. 16: 11 Treating foreigners as native-born- Lev. 19: 34 Ruth as alien and marginalized and welcomed in community- Ruth 2	Kingdom belonging who are like children- Matt. 19: 14 Kingdom as people from all nations- Rev. 7: 9

Theological Perspective

The experience and state of marginality of immigrants presents a coherent message that God seeks to convey in his act of redemption. His act of redemption starts first from his very nature and both migration and marginality are expressions of who he is and what his mission is.

The Centrality of God

Both migration and marginality are expressions of God's call on humanity to make him the central figure. The call of Abraham to take the migration journey to form a nation was a call to faith. The deliverance of the Israelites from Egypt was to manifest God's power to the nations and the concomitant forty-year migration was a daily act of trust in God's provision. In the same manner, their exilic experience was punishment for their act of disobedience of decentering God in their national life. God's commandment for his centrality is core to a covenantal relationship with him. In their deliverance and migration to the promised land, the first four commandments (Exo. 20: 1-11) are expressive enough of God's demand to be at the center of their national life. Jesus delineated the centrality of God in a relational manner through his summary of the commandments (Matt. 22: 36-40).

In this call for God's centrality, it is normative that God's people are placed in a state of marginality through this act of dependence and faith. The writer of Hebrews (Heb. 11) referenced the journeys and experiences of the Old Testament figures as manifestations of faith which calls Christians to journey with God in faith. Yet this is a transformed marginality that is not a product of sin nor human acts of injustice but based on a covenantal relationship. Relational Interactionism provides a framework for understanding this relational marginality. Man's relationship with God stems from God's Triune relationship where there is unity among the three persons of the Trinity. Man's relationship with God proceeds from this unity by being created in his image. Man's existence is never outside of this relationship with the Triune God. It is a transformed marginality as it is in this relationship and dependence where he experiences life (Jn. 10: 10), freedom from sin (Rom. 6: 14), and becomes a slave to righteousness (Rom. 6: 22). Yet, in the centrality of God, he also models marginality where God is the center. God's incarnation in Christ is an act of self-emptying (Phil. 2: 5-11) and a way of life for his people (Jn. 13: 1-17).

In this manner, immigrants can also endure the state of marginality by learning from God's act of marginality (Phil. 2: 5-11). Yet in this experience of marginality, it now becomes relational as it proceeds from one's relationship with the Triune God who is relational in himself. The immigrants' journey is defined as an act of faith in the God who consistently walks with immigrants and who himself became an immigrant. This God must endure marginality in his incarnation, having taken on the form of a servant. God's claim to centrality is distinct for he anchors it on a covenant relationship, first with his chosen people in the Old Testament (2 Sam. 23: 5) and then through a seed of David who ushered in a new covenant (Lk. 22: 20) where God gave the gift of reconciliation and restored fellowship with Him and each other. In this restoration of relationships, God seeks to restore the exiled and marginalized state of man due to sin and bring in a transformed marginality that is anchored on his very nature as a faithful God. Man is then called to live a distinct and honorable life regardless of their conditions on this earth. It is interesting to note how Peter, in his message to Christians in exile, juxtaposed their experience of being foreigners as an archetype of the life of Christians as foreigners in this world. As such, Christians are called to display an honorable way of life requiring that they endure a state of marginality and showing that state as a badge of being Christ-followers (1 Pet. 2: 11-25). The condition of marginality of immigrants is a significant experience that they endure and also a message they bring to all Christ-followers that any experience of marginality is an articulation of God's act of marginality, with such act fulfilling the elevation of the second person of the Trinity into the center of all creation and nations (Phil. 2: 9- 11).

The Justice of God

The centrality of God and the call to a transformed marginality for immigrants do not negate God's demand for justice of their marginal condition. Even as he calls his people to forego the quest for power and centrality, he calls those who shifted to positions of centrality to pursue justice for those in the margins. His call to compassion and justice for the foreigners (Lev. 19: 33-34; Deut. 24: 5) always carries a reminder that his people were once slaves in Egypt. Justice and compassion are then actions derived from previous experience that entails passing it forward. It is then instructive to state at this stage that host and majority cultures are informed that their centrality is derivative. It is derived from God's act of deliverance from their previous state of marginality (in the case of Israel, from their previous state of slavery). Host cultures are called to invite those in the margins into a space of equality and dignity. As stated earlier, God's call for justice demands equality to restore uneven power relations. He then commands not to show partiality to the marginalized (Lev. 19: 15; Deut. 16: 19).

This forward cycle of justice is anchored on God as the only Being that has the claim to centrality. Everyone is reminded that God is the source of justice. In his commandments to show justice and compassion to the foreigners, God consistently concludes his commandments with "I am the Lord your God." Thus, biblical justice is derived from God's nature. In defining biblical justice, Keller claims that "biblical justice is not a set of bullet points or a set of rules and guidelines. It is rooted in the very character of God, and it is the outworking of that character, which is never less than just."[124] This conception of justice is distinct from secular views that equate justice as fairness, as exemplified by John Rawls.[125]

Being rooted in the character of God also means that biblical justice is relational. The horizontal relationship of Relational Interactionism framework also means that God is calling humanity into a new relationship that is not dominated by power, but service (Matt. 20: 20-28); Lk. 22: 24-27) and love (Matt. 22: 39). God seeks a shift from a power-based relationship that is dictated by partiality against the poor and favoritism for the great and into a new relational modality where marginality is the new norm (Matt. 5: 1-12).

The Mission of God

The diaspora missiology framework provides a lens of understanding migration and the consequent marginality as essential to the mission of God. The entry of sin impacted humanity's existence starting from Adam and Eve being driven out from the garden (Gen. 3: 23-24) and Cain's eventual wandering across the face of the earth (Gen. 4: 12). The further breakdown of humanity's relationship with God in the Babel event (Gen. 11: 1-9) led to the fragmentation of cultural relationships and constant displacement. With this fragmentation, displacement, and isolation from God, God's mission is a call to the nations to be gathered under his lordship. His call of Abraham to leave his country and be the father of a nation and an instrument of his blessings to the nations is a manifestation of God's missional framework of the gathering of nations.[126] Wright categorically defined the role of Israel (and the whole testimony of the Old Testament), as being chosen to be a blessing for the nations.[127] What was established with Israel was a missional covenant. In the same manner, Jesus' mission, and that of the Church, is the ingathering of nations.[128] Both Jesus and Paul see their mission work as an "eschatological necessity."[129] In this manner, the mission to the nations or to every cultural, racial, and language group ("*panta ta ethne*") necessitates the understanding of the movement of the gospel among the people on the move.

---

[124] Keller, "Justice in the Bible."
[125] John Rawls, "Justice as Fairness: Political Not Metaphysical," *Philosophy & Public Affairs* 14, no. 3 (1985): 223–51.
[126] Tracy J. McKenzie, "The Hebrew Bible and the Nations," in, Bruce Riley Ashford, ed., *Theology and Practice of Mission: God, The Church, and the Nations* (Nashville, TN: B&H Academic, c. 2011), 146-159.
[127] Christopher J.H. Wright, *The Mission of God: Unlocking the Bible's Grand Narrative* (Downers Grove, Il.: IVP Academic, 2006), 454- 500.
[128] Wright, *The Mission of God*, 501- 530.
[129] Wright, *The Mission of God*, 511.

The movement of peoples is then essential to God's redemptive mission of reconciling humanity back to him by catalyzing these movements to bring his message of redemption to the nations. From this perspective, the Lausanne movement conceptualized diaspora missiology as "a missiological framework for understanding and participating in God's redemptive mission among people living outside their place of origin."[130]

It was mentioned previously that his centrality involves people he called on the migration journey to total dependence on God's leading and provision. While this is a call to a transformed marginality, the very state of marginality of immigrants as an experience of powerlessness already presupposes a missional message. In the Babel event (Gen. 11: 1-9), God's act of scattering and confounding the peoples' language was not just a way of decentering humanity but of fulfilling his pluralistic design for his creation and revealing his greatness to all the nations. Bernhard Anderson rightly claims that "the Babel story has profound significance for a biblical theology of pluralism. First, God's will for his creation is diversity rather than homogeneity."[131] The movement of peoples in all of history should not just be interpreted as a natural phenomenon devoid of this divine plan. Of further affirmation to this divine plan was his intentional act of bringing the gospel into the different languages of people through the Pentecost experience. Pierson identifies three missiological principles in the Pentecost experience. First, God wants people to hear the gospel in their heart language. Second, the whole world is represented symbolically by the Jewish diaspora. And third, it was the fulfillment of Joel's prophesy in Joel 2: 28-29, which was quoted by Peter in Acts 2: 1-21.[132] I disagree with Pierson's claim, however, that the Pentecost was a reversal of Babel in that it was to bring humanity together from the experience of fragmentation and scattering. The revelation of the gospel to the Jewish diaspora was a call that they are being called to receive the gospel and bring that gospel back to the nations. In a way, it is a continuation of the Babel event as an act of purposive scattering to bring the message of redemption to the nations.

This is reflective of Kreitzer's premise that the ethno-linguistic diversity in the Babel event was not a curse.[133] The ethno-linguistic diversity is further to be understood as an acceleration of God's creative process that he commanded his

---

[130] Lausanne Movement, "The Seoul Declaration on Diaspora Missiology," November 14, 2009, https://www.lausanne.org/content/statement/the-seoul-declaration-on-diaspora-missiology.

[131] Bernhard W. Anderson, *From Creation to New Creation: Old Testament Perspectives* (Eugene, Oregon: WIPF and Stock Publishers, 2005), 177.

[132] Pierson E., *The Dynamics of Christian Mission*, 22–23.

[133] Kreitzer, *The Concept of Ethnicity in the Bible,* 134.

people to scatter. Sin and rebellion led humanity to go the opposite way of a "one-world imperial power."[134] Thus:

> The Babel story thus is essential to the concept of created goodness—yet also brokenness—of ethnic diversity. Far from being a curse, implying ethno-linguistic solidarity was a form of judgment to be overcome by redemption, the scattering at Babel was an unmitigated good, because it forced now diversified humankind to obey God's creational commission.[135]

In connecting this to the Pentecost, Kreitzer added that there is a relationship between Babel and Pentecost. Pentecost was not a reversal of Babel but a continuation of God's purpose of restoring languages to "worship and praise the one true God-creator."[136]

In delineating migration as a movement of the gospel to the nations, the state of marginality of immigrants carries with it the message of the Kingdom. While Scripture calls us to show compassion and justice to those who are marginalized, God also points to such marginality as the value of the Kingdom. The experience of marginality is the embodiment of servanthood, of service, of being the least, as hallmarks of the Kingdom. A missiological principle here is that the immigrants' state of marginality is a call towards a new relational space where their powerlessness is a virtue. In the parable of the banquet (Lk. 14: 15-24), Jesus gave reference to the downtrodden and the powerless in society as being invited into the banquet after the rejection of those originally invited. While the parable was a message to Israel of their rejection of the Messiah and an announcement that the offer of salvation is now open to the gentiles, it nevertheless speaks of the foreigners and those who are considered as "unclean" as being invited into a relationship with God. Thus, being in a place of centrality is seen as a hindrance to the acceptance of God's invitation while powerlessness or marginality makes one open to such invitation.

Summary

The reality of migration in the 21st century compels us to see the missiological dimension of this movement of people. Part of this migration journey is the experience of marginality where immigrants face powerlessness in the form of exclusion, discrimination, and marginalization. Yet, biblical and scriptural foundations point to the experience of marginality as woven into the lives of God's people as they migrate whether due to sinfulness, forced displacement, or a response to God's call. In that experience of marginality, God manifests his message of the nature of his Kingdom and his mission. As scripture reveals that

---

[134] Kreitzer, *The Concept of Ethnicity in the Bible*, 136.
[135] Kreitzer, *The Concept of Ethnicity in the Bible*, 137.
[136] Kreitzer, *The Concept of Ethnicity in the Bible*, 338-345.

all God's people are foreigners and exiles on this earth, he calls them to proffer the value of marginality where being his followers means not seeking power but making their condition of powerlessness as an archetype of being under his lordship. To be under God is to be under a relational marginality.

The immigrants are God's missionaries of this relational marginality. Their migration journey and experience of marginality are agencies of God's redemptive purpose of calling people to be subject to his lordship. The next chapter presents the nature of ethnicity as an essential factor of diaspora marginality. It also highlights the fact that ethnicity is also essential to God's redemptive purpose.

CHAPTER 5

NATURE OF ETHNICITY: ITS ROLE IN MARGINALITY AND ITS MISSIOLOGICAL PURPOSE

Introduction

The experience of marginality of many people groups is becoming pronounced with the movement of peoples crossing geographic boundaries and creating ethnic divisions. Diaspora marginality is first and foremost an issue of ethnic or racial inequality. Uneven power relations, cultural marginalization, and racial discrimination are directed to the ethnic otherness of diaspora peoples. This is evident in the experience of diaspora visible minorities in Canada and other Caucasian-dominated nations. Marginality is seen as a condition of being excluded, alienated, and in the geographic and economic periphery of the host nation.

Biblically, scripturally and theologically, the prevailing racism and discrimination are testaments to the impact of sin on human relations. Man's rebellion with God and the destruction of the relationship with the Triune God distorted humanity's relationship with each other. A concomitant effect of sin is ethnic inequality where other people groups are perceived as of lower status. The current issue of racism is one significant expression of sin. Ethnicity, however, is central to God's design for plurality and his redemptive purpose for the nations.

The Meaning of *Ethnos*

Ethnicity is not a term that could just be defined directly without nuances. Kreitzer provided a meaningful delineation of different social science perspectives by looking at different theories of ethnicity.[137] One theory is Primordialism which views ethnicity as a bounded set of cultural traits within a sealed boundary. It looks at ethnicity as a fixed, unchangeable identity.[138] Another social theory of ethnicity is Instrumentalism. In contrast to Primordialism, Instrumentalism does not believe in the constant, unchanging nature of culture but changes according to group needs for collective social and political action. Kreitzer delineated the Marxian influence om Instrumentalism where culture is seen as moldable. "Ethnic identity, thus, according to instrumentalism is collective and involves communication structured by the surrounding society. Such identity is always changing though it may include a

---

[137] Kreitzer, *The Concept of Ethnicity in the Bible*, 23–37.
[138] Kreitzer, *The Concept of Ethnicity in the Bible*. 24–27.

pragmatically useful, socially created myth of primordial immutability."[139] Another theory of ethnicity is Social Constructionism. "Ethnicity is actually the product of human construction and is something that evolves over time. In the process, it is constantly redefining itself and being redefined in interaction with other groups."[140]

Each of the theories has substantial contribution to the development of the concept. Within this continuum, Stallard is helpful in integrating the values of these theories by analyzing the thoughts of Jonathan Hall and Eric Barreto.[141] Hall identified three core elements of ethnicity: putative subscription to a myth of common descent and kinship, association with a specific boundary, and sense of shared history.[142] Barreto seems to refer to these elements when he defined ethnicity as "a socially constructed, discursive, pliable claim to be a group of people defined around myths of putative commonality of kinship or ancestry including origins, language, culture, religion, geography, and other organizing principles."[143]

In reflecting on the theories of ethnicity that range from a fixed to a socially constructed state, these conceptions of Hall and Barreto provide integrated meaning. Thus, Stallard opined that Barreto's definition "is helpful because it recognizes ethnicity as both fixed and fluid. It is something that can be negotiated as it is socially constructed." [144]

It is then necessary to determine the theological and missiological perspectives and implications of the concept. A common English translation of the Greek word *ethnos* is nation (plural, *ethne*) as found in most English Bible translations (e.g., Matt. 28: 19). The meaning of the word, however, is contextual. A white paper by Luis Bush that is based on his email communication with the Content Innovation Team of the Logos Bible Software revealed that as to the use of *ethnos* in the New Testament, the term is translated as nation, 63 times, people, 6 times, pagan, 6 times, and country and heathen, one time.[145] In focusing on Matthew 28: 19, Bush notes that the CIT

---

[139] Kreitzer, *The Concept of Ethnicity in the Bible.* 24–27.

[140] Kreitzer, *The Concept of Ethnicity in the Bible.* 30.

[141] Stephen Christian Stallard, "The Development of Multicultural Teams in the Book of Acts: A Model with Application to Urban North America" (PhD Dissertation, Southeastern Baptist Theological Seminary, 2020), 11–13.

[142] Jonathan Hall, *Hellenicity: Between Ethnicity and Culture* (Chicago: University of Chicago Press, 2002), 9.

[143] Eric Barreto, *Ethnic Negotiations: The Function of Race and Ethnicity in Acts 16* (Tübingen: Mohr Siebeck, 2010), 27.

[144] Stallard, "The Development of Multicultural Teams," 13.

[145] Luis Bush, "The Meaning of Ethne in Matthew 28:19," https://www.missionfrontiers.org/issue/article/the-meaning-of-ethne-in-matthew-2819.

analysis that the use of *"panta ta ethne"* refers to peoples other than Israel and is reflective of the use in the Abrahamic promise such as in Genesis 18: 18, which is translated also as *"panta ta ethne"* in the Septuagint.[146] In a sense, these are "those who do not belong to groups professing faith in the God of Israel."[147] Thus, the use of nation (*ethnos*) or nations (*ethne*) in the Bible is directed to those who are not part of the nation of Israel and don't profess the God of Israel. Generally, this coincides with the Hebrew concept of foreigner or *goyim*.[148] The application of the terms "heathen, gentiles, pagans" in this concept of *goyim* tends to reinforce the missiological implication of its usage where God's call to Israel to be a blessing to the nations is to include these nations in God's sphere of sovereignty in the Old Testament context, and the target of discipleship in the New Testament.

This word analysis expresses the meaning of nations as a missiological objective of God to reveal his glory and redemptive purpose to the nations. In connecting the meaning of *"panta ta ethne"* in both the Abrahamic promise and the Great Commission, Wright rightly delineates that "this dynamic narrative of God's saving purpose for all nations in Abraham is the heart of the gospel as announced in the scriptures."[149]

The concept of *ethnos* in the Bible is different than what we currently know it as a political entity with geographic boundaries and governance structure. The closest modern equivalent is an ethnic group. Davis's study to come up with a Biblical Theology of ethnicity states that "our modern use of 'ethnic group' corresponds roughly to the biblical concepts of 'nations,' 'families,' and peoples.'"[150] Our English term ethnic is in fact from the Greek *ethnos* and originally meant a number of people living together as a tribe, a people, a nation, or group."[151]

The modern term adapted in missiological circles is "people group" which is described as those belonging to the same ethnicity.[152] Thus, the biblical *ethnos* (nation) corresponds to the definition of ethnicity as "classification of a person or persons into a particular group based on factors such as physical

---

[146] Bush, "The Meaning of Ethne."

[147] Bush, "The Meaning of Ethne."

[148] Bible.org, "What Does 'Nation, Kindred, Tongue and People' in Rev. 14 Mean?," January 1, 2001, https://bible.org/question/what-does-%E2%80%9Cnation-kindred-tongue-and-people%E2%80%9D-rev-14-mean.

[149] Wright, *The Mission of God*, 193.

[150] Ken L. Davis, "Building a Biblical Theology of Ethnicity for Global Mission," *The Journal of Ministry & Theology*, Fall 2003, 92.

[151] Davis, "Building a Biblical Theology of Ethnicity for Global Mission," 92.

[152] Ralph Winter alludes to this in his development of the concept of "unreached peoples." See Ralph Winter, "Unreached Peoples: The Development of the Concept," in, *International Journal of Frontier Missions*, vol. 1 no. 2 (1984): 129- 161.

characteristics (e.g., skin color, facial characteristics, body shape); cultural identity (e.g., language or dialect, religion), or geographic origin."[153]

Ethnic Inequality in the Bible

There is a plethora of evidence of ethnic discrimination in the Bible based on the foreigner status of other ethnic groups who chose to live with the Israelites. The issue of alienation and discrimination in the Old Testament is imbedded in the stories of biblical personages as well as history of Israel as a nation. As a starting point, The Old Testament concept of aliens or strangers is delineated in the Hebrew word for stranger which is "ger."[154] This is interchangeably translated as alien, sojourner or stranger. Thus, a "ger" is the one residing in a culture different from his own without the benefits of families or citizenship rights. The ministry to foreigners is a central call of God in the Old Testament. In fact, the commandment to love the alien is repeated 36 times. God has always been concerned about the plight of the poor and the powerless. Thus, "ger" is frequently mentioned with other defenseless groups, such as the poor, the widows, and the orphans (Deut. 10:18; Jer. 2: 26). Such provision for loving the foreigners reveal the reality of their experience of oppression, injustice, and marginalization of other ethnic groups within the Jewish society, leading to such legal requirements for their fair and just treatment.

Other biblical entries that speak of ethnicity as a basis for inequality could be gleaned from these passages:

- Genesis 28: 1-19- Isaac's wife requiring Jacob not to marry a Canaanite.
- Deuteronomy 23: 7- Law against discrimination of Edomites and Egyptians.
- John 4: 9- Jews' disdain of Samaritans.
- Galatians 2: 11-14- Paul's argument against Peter on Jewish distinction.

In reflecting on Paul's argument with Peter in Galatians 2: 11-14, it has to be contextualized in his thesis of inclusive salvation that God's grace is sufficient for all. He further added in Galatians 3: 28 of the equality of all peoples in Christ. Campbell, in his study of Romans, posits that Paul's argument is not against ethnic distinction but discrimination.[155] "What Paul opposes is the hostility that emerges from a failure to recognize and accept the other in their

---

[153] Donald R. Jacobs, "Ethnicity," in, A Scott Moreau, ed., *Evangelical Dictionary of World Missions* (Grand Rapids, Michigan: Baker Books, 2000), 323.

[154] Brenda Thompson, "An Overview of Old Testament Principles on Reaching the Refugees in Our Midst," *International Journal of Frontier Missions* 2, no. 4 (October 1985): 363–68.

[155] William S. Campbell, "Differentiation and Discrimination in Paul's Ethnic Discourse," *Transformation* 30, no. 3 (July 2013): 157–268.

distinctive identity."[156] Keller added to this by claiming that Paul's argument is not just saying that racism is sin but is the product of rejection of the gospel and "a return to justification by our moral efforts."[157] Thus, in claiming that ethnicity does not make any difference in Christ, he was not downplaying ethnic identity but affirming that such ethnic identity does not equate to unequal status in Christ.

Missiology of Ethnicity: Biblical and Scriptural Perspectives

The concept of nations as referring to people groups, particularly those who don't profess the God of Israel has a clear missiological connotation. Yet what needs to be emphasized as well is that tied to God's mission to the nations of revealing himself and fulfilling his redemptive plan, ethnicity is reflective of his nature and his pluralistic design for his creation. A biblical survey is essential in delineating God's purpose for the nations and how this fit into his overall design for his creation. It is this intersection between mission and pluralism that reverberates in all of scripture.

The Old Testament

The Pluralistic Purpose of Ethnicity

The creation story in Genesis provides a significant foundation for God's purpose for ethnicity. Of interest is that the diversity of his creation stems essentially from his nature. It is no coincidence that God is referred to in a plural sense (Gen. 1: 26). Aside from the diversity of creatures (Gen. 1: 20-25), mankind as the crown of his creation was also created in plurality (Gen. 1: 27). His desire for human diversity is an essential part of his creative process and design with the commandment for humanity to fill the earth. He gave them a cultural mandate of exercising responsibility to subdue the earth (Gen. 1: 26-30). Ashford and Bridger noted that central to the provision of culture-making capacities is God's establishment of cultures,[158] which is one of the markers of ethnicity. Such command to fill the earth is commensurate with other biblical attributions to God's purpose for scattering people (Gen. 9: 7; Deut. 32: 28; Acts 19: 26). Even humanity's rebellion and the consequent fall fulfilled God's scattering of mankind through migration, first through Adam and Eve being driven out of the garden (Gen. 3: 23-24) and Cain's wandering (Gen. 4: 12-16).

---

[156] Campbell, "Differentiation and Discrimination," 157.
[157] Timothy Keller, "The Bible and Race," *Life in the Gospel*, March 2020, https://quarterly.gospelinlife.com/the-bible-and-race/.
[158] Bruce Ashford and Scott Bridger, "Missiological Method," in *Missiology: An Introduction to the Foundations, History, and Strategies of World Missions*, ed. John Mark Terry (Nashville, TN: B & H Academic, 2015), 37.

The genealogy in Genesis 5 is not merely to delineate Adam's family line but to express the formation of families that would connect with the formation of nations in Genesis 9 and 10.

After the fall, God's movement for diversity is commensurate with the migration of humanity as well as his desire to bring his glory and sovereignty to the nations or people groups. The following texts bear this out:

- Genesis 5: 1-2- God created mankind as male and female.
- Genesis 9: 19- Sons of Noah as fathers of nations.
- Genesis 10- Table of nations.

Of particular interest in this book is how the table of nations in chapter 10 defined key characteristics or identifying markers of ethnicity with land, language, and family repeated three times (Gen. 10: 5, 20, and 31). Thus, to be part of an ethnic group is to share a common geographic location, language, and family. Davis claims that "one of God's gifts to mankind, it seems, is to be included in a particular group of people—this gives a sense of belonging, identity, and security."[159]

From Genesis 1 to 10, there is this pervading theme of his establishing nations or people groups by scattering them to fill the earth as manifested by his command to mankind (Gen. 1: 28) and the family of Noah (Gen. 9: 7). In this diversity of people groups, God also maintains the unity of mankind even in spite of the fall and their rebellion. God intended for unity even in the context of ethnic diversity. Such unity is expressed by God through common speech and language (Gen.11: 1). Thus, the scattering of people was not an avenue for division but diversity. While it was God's intent for the scattering of peoples to form nations, humanity went in the opposite direction and expressed their sinfulness and rebellion through re-gathering and centralization (Gen. 11: 1-4). The confusion of language further reinforces diversity, with language as one of the essential features of ethnicity.

The Missiological Purpose of Ethnicity

There is a significant shift in focus from God's desire to form nations towards a specific clan starting in Genesis 12 with the attention given to Abraham and his descendants. With people groups scattered into different geographic locations, the attention on one nation does not deviate from God's overall design to reveal himself to the nations and fulfill his redemptive plan. This shift signifies a movement from God's overall intent to form and scatter nations towards a missiological purpose of redeeming these nations. God's blessing to Abraham is intended to bless all nations (Gen. 12: 2; Gen. 18: 18; 22: 18; 26: 4). Essex notes

---

[159] Davis, "Building a Biblical Theology of Ethnicity for Global Mission," 95.

that the Hebrew term used in these passages is *"goyim."*[160] As mentioned earlier, this is translated as *"panta ta ethne"* in the Septuagint. In this context, the blessing to all nations through Abraham is a manifestation of God's desire to redeem the rebellious nations through one nation that is distinct from the nations. For Essex, the call of Abraham to leave his land is to leave his nation that had been part of the rebellion against God.[161] "Thus, the Lord called Abraham to renounce his identification with the nations who were in rebellion against Him."[162]

The call of the nation of Israel to bless the nations signifies key aspects of God's redemptive purpose. First, Israel is called to be a kingdom of priests and a holy nation to be an expression of God's sovereignty (Exo. 19: 3-6). Second, this call is a call to be a blessing to the nations. "As a holy priest-nation, they were to mediate between God and the other ethnic nations (the Gentiles), making them acceptable to God and sharing with them all that God was revealing. They were his representatives to the world's peoples. Here, then, was Israel's ministry and "missionary calling."[163] And third, there is a moral dimension to this calling. Israel is to be a model to other nations of God's righteousness through its obedience to his commandments (Deut. 4: 5-8).[164] The missionary calling of Israel to be a blessing to the nations is evident in the Old Testament (e.g., Josh. 4: 24; Isa. 60: 1-3; Ps. 96: 3; 1 Chr. 16: 8-9; Zech. 8: 20-23; Eze. 37: 27-28; Mic. 4: 1-3). The formation of Israel as a nation shows a continuity of God's purpose for the nation starting from the Abrahamic covenant to the Davidic covenant that fulfills God's messianic plan (2 Sam. 7 and 1 Chr. 17). Even with the destruction of the kingdom, the messianic line through David is fulfilled in Jesus Christ, and thus confirms the special call of Israel to be a nation where God's redemptive purpose for the nations is fulfilled.

What is the purpose of ethnicity in God's redemptive plan? There is no question about his pluralistic design for his creation, his sovereignty over all nations, and his redemptive purpose for all people groups. We claim, however, that ethnicity is his vehicle for his salvific message. In going back to Genesis 11: 1-9, his scattering of people groups into different geographic locations was not just a concern of man's tendency or concentration. Man's rebellion and concomitant confusion of language necessitates contextual revelation and contextual mission. God's salvific plan is contextual given the location and language diversity. As God designed diversity, it only means that he wants his people to know him and worship him in their heart language and cultural

---

[160] Keith H. Essex, "The Abrahamic Covenant," *The Masters Seminary Journal* 10, no. 2 (Fall 1999): 198.
[161] Essex, "The Abrahamic Covenant," 197.
[162] Essex, "The Abrahamic Covenant," 197.
[163] Davis, "Building a Biblical Theology of Ethnicity for Global Mission," 97–98.
[164] Davis, "Building a Biblical Theology of Ethnicity for Global Mission," 98.

expressions. These cultural expressions are part of God's cultural mandate (Gen. 1: 26-30). "God established culture when he created his imagers with culture-making capacities."[165] The cultural mandate is a responsibility to create and at the same time a gift to be creative. While this is obvious, what is not highlighted frequently is that this gift to create is shaped and influenced by the social and environmental context where an individual or human community is situated. The result of this contextual creative response is a unique and diverse set of cultural flourishing all over the world. Thus, ethnicity is both a product and furtherance of God's plan for diversity, and at the same time to establish mission clarity so that people groups understand his redemptive purpose in their cultural context and heart language. As ethnicity is central to God's plan for diversity, it is then central to his plan to know his Triune identity. The Trinity expresses God's unity in his diversity. The Trinity is "a vision of how humanity should be."[166]

New Testament

Ethnicity in the Gospels

Ethnicity as an expression of God's desire for diversity as well as its role in his mission is manifested in the New Testament. Of note is how the New Testament starts with the genealogy of Jesus that traces his lineage from Abraham (Matt. 1). This only delineates Jesus as the fulfillment of both the Abrahamic covenant and the Davidic covenant. In both cases, this affirms Jesus' ministry and salvific act as continuity of God's desire to call all nations under his sovereignty and receive his redemption.

It is obvious, however, that Jesus' message is more directed towards a rebuke of Israel. A stated in both the Abrahamic and Davidic covenant, Israel is called to be a blessing to the nations. The New Testament era, however, shows a shift in perspective of the people of Israel as having an exclusive claim to God's blessing. Thus, Jesus' rebuke of the Pharisees and other religious leaders' insistence on the fulfillment of the letter of the law (Matt. 23; Lk. 11: 39-54) manifests the latter's claim that the fulfillment of these laws expresses their claim of God's grace. Jesus' shift to include non-Jews in his call for salvation reaffirms God's kingdom as reserved for the nations, to wit:

- Matt. 22: 1-14- Parable of the Banquet as an invitation for all.
- Lk. 10: 25-37- Parable of the Good Samaritan.
- Jn. 4: 1-42- The Samaritan Woman at the Well.

---

[165] Ashford and Bridger, "Missiological Method," 37.
[166] Fr. Mark Gatto, "The Holy Trinity: A Vision of How Humanity Should Be," June 16, 2019, https://www.catherineofsienachurch.ca/the-holy-trinity-a-vision-of-how-humanity-should-live/.

- Mk. 7: 24-30- Healing of the Syrophoenician woman's daughter.

While these are just a few of the numerous gospel narratives of Jesus' acts and teachings of the inclusive nature of God's grace, these delineate the blessing of salvation as available to all. The inclusive nature of God's kingdom is best captured in the Great Commission's (Matt. 28: 16-20) by affirming God's plan of salvation for *"panta ta ethne."* Jesus' intent is fulfilling the Abrahamic and Davidic covenant on the role of Israel to be a blessing to the nations. He is acutely aware of his messianic role for the nations, not only through his constant inclusion of non-Jews and those outside of Jewish mainstream society (e.g., poor, sinners, lepers) as an expression that God's grace, but of the universal nature of salvation through his salvific act. Central to his understanding of his claim to be the Messiah (Luke 4: 18, 19) by quoting Isaiah 61: 1-2, is not just the affirmation to include the marginalized. What should not be missed is that, in the Jewish' rejection of his messianic claim, he referenced foreigners in verses 26 and 27 as the ones that showed compassion (Elijah's experience) and were shown compassion as well (Elisha's experience). Jesus was proclaiming that his ministry was for all nations. Jesus' life and teachings are expressions of the outward movement of the gospel.

Ethnicity in the Book of Acts

Essential to this is also his desire for people to respond to his salvific act through their specific ethnic identity. While outside of the four gospels, the best place to understand Jesus' intent is the Lukan Great Commission (Acts 1:8). The unique aspect of the Lukan Great Commission is not just its reflection of the Great Commission in Matthew 28: 16-20 of calling the disciples to be witnesses to the ends of the earth but of the empowerment of the Holy Spirit to fulfill this purpose. This was realized in Acts 2 at the time of Pentecost when the Holy Spirit enabled the disciples to speak in different languages and be understood by God-fearing Jews from other nations. The Spirit's first work at the Pentecost was to translate the gospel into different languages.[167] The empowering of the Holy Spirit manifests God's act of affirming man's common humanity amid their diversity. Of unique interest is the mention of specific people groups in verses 9 to 11. The Pentecost provided the key to the role of ethnicity in God's salvific act by enabling the disciples to speak in different languages and mentioning specific people groups or ethnicities, thus becoming a model to "communicate the Good News of the mighty Acts of God in Christ, to every people in their heart language and culture."[168] As the Babel experience resulted in confusion to intentionally scatter people, the Pentecost is a marker of God's desire to bring back people into unity and affirm his sovereignty over all nations. It was both a

---

[167] Howell M. and Paris W., *Introducing Cultural Anthropology*, 254.
[168] Pierson, *The Dynamics of Christian Mission*, 23.

missiological event of spreading the gospel to different people groups and an eschatological event of the ingathering of nations. At the Pentecost, God came down in blessing and not in judgment.[169]

Ethnicity in God's kingdom as manifested by such eschatological event, and his desire to let people respond to his redemptive plan in their distinct ethnicity, delineates his love for diversity and valuing of ethnic identity. God's gift of dividing humanity into nations and setting specific boundaries is reflected in Paul's message on the Areopagus (Acts 17: 26). Interestingly, Paul's message reflects his purpose of setting ethnic boundaries in the Old Testament (Deut. 32: 28). For Davis, "ethnic identity appears to be an inevitable consequence of God's providence."[170] Paul was not just affirming the value of ethnic identity in God's kingdom. He was also a significant instrument of God in delineating ethnic identity for gospel transmission to the nations. It is not by coincidence that Paul was instrumental in breaking down the barriers to spread the gospel from the Jews to the nations owing to his Jewish and Hellenistic backgrounds. Essential to Paul's strategy is his affirmation of culture as a way for the gospel to be understood in the context of the hearers. He made use of his Jewish and Hellenistic backgrounds to convey the gospel, using cultural images and terminologies in doing so.[171]

Ethnicity in Pauline Teachings

Paul's teaching methods are not just about fulfilling God's desire to enable nations to respond to his redemptive plan in their specific context but also about focusing on the redeeming power of the gospel to transform the culture of people groups. The gospel is the heart of Paul's letters and teachings. All his teachings and letters are ways of conveying that the gospel renews and transforms every ethnic group and their culture. In Flemming's view of Paul's teachings, the understanding of Christian faith is not focused on timeless theological truth or principle but contingent on a historical happening: the crucifixion and resurrection of Jesus.[172] In this regard, "God's saving action in the death and resurrection of Christ becomes an experienced reality (Gal. 4: 4-7)."[173] Thus, ethnic identity enables people groups to understand and respond to the historical particularity of God's saving grace. Paul could claim that Christ's incarnation is a matter of God involved in human history and experience so that he could assume his lordship over every human reality and sinfulness (Phil. 2: 5-11). It is no wonder that Paul concludes this hymn with

---

[169] Keller, "The Bible and Race."
[170] Davis, "Building a Biblical Theology of Ethnicity for Global Mission," 100.
[171] Dean Flemming, *Contextualization in the New Testament: Patterns for Theology and Mission* (Downers Grove, Il.: AVP Academic, 2009), 56-181.
[172] Flemming, *Contextualization in the New Testament*, 94.
[173] Flemming, *Contextualization in the New Testament*, 103.

the acknowledgment of Christ's lordship by every tongue. It should be noted that the verse does not only allude to nations. To understand the verse, the words "tongue" and "confess" need to be understood together. The reference to "tongue" (*glossa*) includes all beings and the meaning of "confess" (*exomologeo*) literally means speaking the same thing that another speaks.[174] A Greek word study, however, delineates that "tongue" also refers to "language."[175] This is also the same word used in the day of the Pentecost when the disciples spoke "with other tongues" (Acts 2: 4) and such tongue refers to human languages (Acts 2: 8). In this sense, "every tongue" refers to the diversity of human languages that can have the same proclamation of the lordship of Christ. In Paul, Christ's incarnation is affirming God's purpose of ethnic identity and diversity as means of pluralistic expressions of worship.

Ethnicity and the Ingathering of Nations in Revelation

Such proclamation of all nations or people groups of the lordship of Christ is expressed in the ingathering of nations (Rev. 7: 9). Of particular interest is that this culmination of God's salvation plan specifically delineates each ethnicity or people group to be present and represented. Thus, while Paul's message and ministry revolve around the spread of the gospel to the nations, the eschatological purpose is not lost in his teachings. Such eschatological purpose is nowhere expressed categorically than in Revelations where God reveals his glory to all nations and gathers them into his kingdom (Rev. 7: 9; 14: 6; 21: 24-28).

In delineating nation, tribe, language, and people in Revelation, this must be an emphasis of all people groups based on their ethnic identities. Some of the terms have already been defined earlier:

- nation (*ethnos*)- mostly equivalent to the Hebrew "*goyim*" or foreigners, gentiles; people who don't yet recognize the God of Israel.
- Language or tongue (*glossa*)- a reference to languages spoken by different people groups or "a synonym for a group of people by their particular language or even dialect."[176]

---

[174] "Philippians 2:11 Commentary," *Precept Austin*, n.d., https://www.preceptaustin.org/philippians_211_commentary.

[175] "The Greek Word 'Glossa,'" *Online Greek Word Study* (blog), March 29, 2016, https://www.bumchecks.com/biblecommentary/2016/03/29/the-greek-word-glossa/.

[176] "What Does 'Nation, Kindred, Tongue and People' in Rev. 14 Mean?," *Bible.org*, January 1, 2001, https://bible.org/question/what-does-%E2%80%9Cnation-kindred-tongue-and-people%E2%80%9D-rev-14-mean.

Additional terms should be defined:
- Tribe (*Phune*)- nation of people (Matt. 24:30; Rev. 1:7) or "a smaller group within a particular nation." [177]
- People (*Laos*)- "people as a nation."[178]

In the use and combination of these terminologies, these are to convey the totality of God's salvific act for all peoples. These also emphasize the diversity of God's people because of his scattering and seeks to maintain such diversity and delineates ethnic identities as markers of such diversity. In a sense, the book of Revelation marks the "eschatological ultimacy"[179] of God's covenant of blessing all nations.

The biblical survey and word study show the arc of God's redemptive purpose for the nations from his original intent of scattering towards his ultimate objective in the eschatological gathering. It is beyond the scope of the paper to discuss if all peoples from all nations will be included in his salvific plan.[180]

A Theology of Ethnicity

The word study of ethnicity and biblical survey provide key direction in formulating a theology of ethnicity. Theology is the understanding of our 'knowledge of God.[181] In this regard, theologizing is the act of understanding a phenomenon from the perspective of God and his purpose as revealed in scripture. Ethnicity is not just a biological, social, and cultural construct but stems from God's purpose for humanity.

Ethnicity as Expression of God's Triune Nature

The concept of ethnicity as a reflection of plurality and its role in God's mission needs to be anchored on the nature of God himself. As an expression of diversity and pluralism in creation, the origin of diversity is not to be seen from creation but the creator himself. In the creation story, the diverse nature of creation stems from the Triune God. Thus, Davis notes that:

---

[177] "What Does 'Nation, Kindred, Tongue and People' in Rev. 14 Mean?"
[178] "What Does 'Nation, Kindred, Tongue and People' in Rev. 14 Mean?"
[179] As used by Richard Bauckham, *The Theology of the Book of Revelation* (Cambridge: Cambridge University Press, 1993), 103.
[180] For a full treatment of the subject, see Dave Mathewson, "The Destiny of the Nations in Revelation 21:1-22:5: A Reconsideration," *Tyndale Bulletin* 53, no. 1 (2002): 121–42.
[181] See Erik Thoennes, "What Is Theology?", *The Good Book Blog - Talbot School of Theology Faculty Blog*, May 16, 2016, https://www.biola.edu/blogs/good-book-blog/2016/what-is-theology.

"The first three chapters of Genesis also reveal a Triune God who creates mankind in His image, capable of relationships. The three persons of the Godhead commune among themselves ("let us make man") and in turn seek out man's unrequited love. Genesis shows that humanity was created for being in a communion that both reflects and glorifies the Triune communion."[182]

In delineating plurality as stemming from the Triune God, the idea of harmony and unity is essential to the Trinity. Without leading into arguments of the expression of the Trinity in the Old Testament, suffice it to say that the consistency of scripture naturally leads us to conclude Genesis 1: 26 as an expression of a God who is in "Triune communion." And it is from this unity and plurality of the Triune God that his creation of mankind and the rest of creation proceeds as a pluralistic endeavor and that there is diversity in this creation (Gen. 1: 26-27).

Ethnicity as an expression of God's creative process for human diversity stems from his plurality. The Triune God manifests his nature in plurality with each person of the Trinity distinct and with a specific purpose in his creative process and salvific act. Every person of the Trinity is equal. As there is unity in God's plurality, so is there unity between God and his creation and that his creation reflects its creator. Thus, ethnic diversity is a manifestation and expression of God's plurality. From this pluralistic nature of God also derives the nature of ethnic diversity and identity. As humanity comes from a Triune God who is in perfect unity, then humanity is also created in unity amid diversity. Humanity is God's offspring and thus every "*ethnos*" is equal. In his creative process, he created one man to be the progenitor of all nations (Acts. 17: 26). The origins of humanity as coming from one ancestry has never been in doubt even in the sciences.[183] His creation of mankind is also an act of plurality (Gen. 1: 27). Thus, ethnic diversity and plurality are a result of a pluralistic God.

Human diversity and ethnicity could only flourish when it is anchored in relationship with God. Human relationships become also united when such unity with God is established. One of the key paradigms in studying the role of ethnicity in God's mission is Wan's Relational Realism model. Relational Realism is "the systematic understanding that 'reality is primarily based on the 'vertical relationship' between God and the created world and secondarily 'horizontal relationship' with the created order."[184] From this trinitarian relationship proceeds God's relationship with his creation (Economic Trinity) or what the paradigm calls the vertical relationship. Thus, reality is "based on

---

[182] Davis, "Building a Biblical Theology of Ethnicity for Global Mission," 94.

[183] See Ashley Montagu, *Man's Most Dangerous Myth: The Fallacy of Race*, 5th ed. (London: Oxford University Press, 1974).

[184] Wan and Hedinger, *Relational Missionary Training*, 34.

the interactive relationships between Divine Creator Being (Triune God) and created beings (people and other spirit beings)."[185]

In delineating Relational Realism as a framework in understanding the role of ethnicity in God's mission, a key point is to be emphasized, namely, ethnicity leads to division and inequality when such ethnic identity is not anchored on the God who maintains perfect unity of the three persons of the Trinity. The Babel experience is the result of de-anchoring human identity from the Triune God.

Ethnicity as Part of God's Creative Process

God's formation of nations and the consequent diverse ethnic identities is a continuation of his creative process. As creation is diverse, so is his formation of humanity (Gen. 1: 27). His command to increase in number and populate the earth (Gen. 1: 28; Gen. 9: 7) resulted in the formation of nations by specifying their boundaries (Deut. 32: 28; Acts 17: 26). As scattering was his original intent, ethnic diversity is consequently his plan rather than the result of sin. Even after the flood and the Babel event, his desire is the formation of nations, and his confounding of languages, are acts of providence rather than punishment.

The cultural mandate (Gen. 1: 28-30) is also a reflection of man created in the image of God as his co-creator. In this cultural mandate, the formation of different ethnic cultures is corollary to his creation of boundaries (Deut. 32: 28; Acts 17: 26) which God designs to express different worship expressions. It is evident in this case that missions to the nations need to convey affirmations of these cultural differences in worship expressions. The tendency of missionary work that is anchored on a Western cultural lens is repugnant to God's process of creative delegation. The act of delegation entails the consistency of the relationship between the delegator to the ones being delegated. This role is not independent of nor free from the power of God who delegates such creative responsibility. Sin is a manifestation of this relational co-creative process.

Ethnicity as Expression of God's Missionary Character

God designed and desired his creation to be in a relationship with him. His formation of nations is to make himself known to these nations, and in man's disobedience, God seeks to reconcile and redeem them to be under his lordship and sovereignty. In his design of redemption, he revels in the plurality of worship, where different people groups express varieties of forms of faith and even faith communities. It should be noted as well that the incarnation is an expression of God's contextual revelation and mission and desires his followers

---

[185] Wan and Hedinger, "Transformative Ministry for the Majority World Context," 4.

to follow this incarnational path in mission. With diverse people groups, it is but natural that his message of salvation needs to tailor to specific ethnic and cultural contexts. For Ott, Strauss, and Tennent, "any theology of mission is incomplete until it speaks of the gospel's penetration into every aspect of a people's life and worldview."[186] Ashford and Bridger added to this by claiming that "culture is the God-given matrix within which he desires his people to continually translate the faith faithfully and meaningfully for future generations."[187]

Essential to this missionary character of God is the fulfillment of his eschatological kingdom that draws all people groups to worship him. His plan to bless all nations culminates in this ingathering of all nations, people groups, and languages. "The Lord himself is the missionary who ultimately gathers and rescues, not simply the dispersed of Israel, but also people from all nations so that they may see his glory. The final goal of mission, then, is the glory of God, that he may be known and honored for who he is."[188] His desire is to unite all people groups in relationship with him. In the process, human diversity reflects not only God's pluralistic nature but defines the relational nature of all human interaction amid their distinctiveness.

Summary

The ethnic identity of diaspora visible minorities is crucial in understanding their condition and experience of marginality. Scripturally and theologically, the prevailing racism and discrimination are testaments to the impact of sin on human relations that distorted God's purpose for ethnic diversity. While ethnicity is a factor in marginality, it is important to delineate that ethnicity is essential in God's creative and missiological purpose for humanity.

---

[186] Craig Ott, Stephen J. Strauss, and Timothy C. Tennent, *Encountering Theology of Mission: Biblical Foundations, Historical Developments, and Contemporary Issues* (Grand Rapids: Baker Academic, 2010), 265.

[187] Ashford and Bridger, "Missiological Method," 35.

[188] Davis, "Building a Biblical Theology of Ethnicity for Global Mission," 106.

CHAPTER 6

ETHNICITY AND NATURE OF MARGINALITY OF DIASPORA VISIBLE MINORITIES IN CANADA

Introduction

As delineated in chapter 5, ethnicity is a central factor in diaspora marginality but also an essential element of God's redemptive purpose for the nations. The reality of marginality due to ethnicity can best be understood in a specific context. For this reason, this chapter looks at the ethnicity and nature of marginality of diaspora visible minorities in Canada. Canada is a unique contextual placement of ethnic marginality due to its multicultural makeup and the only country where multiculturalism is an avowed government policy. An examination of concepts is also proffered in this chapter to provide further clarity of how these concepts are understood in this book.

A Review of Concepts

Visible Minority

The concept of visible minority was first coined by the Canadian activist Kay Livingstone "in discussing the socio-political inequalities experienced by non-white minorities."[189] This was adopted by the Commission on Equity in Employment leading to the passage of the Employment Equity Act in 1986, and subsequently legislated in 1995.[190] Its purpose is to "achieve equality in the workplace so that no person shall be denied employment opportunities or benefits for reasons unrelated to ability and, in the fulfilment of that goal, to correct the conditions of disadvantage in employment experienced by women, Aboriginal peoples, persons with disabilities and members of visible minorities by giving effect to the principle that employment equity means more than treating persons in the same way but also requires special measures and the accommodation of differences."[191] Statistics Canada used the term since 1986 to adopt this concept as part of delineating Canadian demographics. As stated earlier, Statistics Canada defines visible minorities as "persons, other than

---

[189] Clayton Ma, "Visible Minority," *The Canadian Encyclopedia*, May 5, 2021, https://www.thecanadianencyclopedia.ca/en/article/minorite-visible.
[190] Ma, "Visible Minority."
[191] "Employment Equity Act," December 15, 1995, https://laws-lois.justice.gc.ca/eng/acts/E-5.401/page-1.html#h-215135.

Aboriginal peoples, who are non-Caucasian in race or non-white in color."[192] The visible minority population consists mainly of South Asians, Chinese, Black, Filipino, Latin American, Arab, Southeast Asian, West Asian, Korean, and Japanese.[193] Currently, visible minorities make up 60.2% of first-generation Canadians.[194] "The qualifier "visible" was added to single out newer immigrant minorities from both Aboriginal Canadians and other minority groups distinguishable by language (French vs. English) and religion (Catholics vs. Protestants), which in some cases are "invisible" traits."[195]

The use of the term "visible minority" as applied to these ethnicities is to make a distinction of newer immigrants of non-white or non-Caucasian backgrounds and is thereby purely descriptive. The Ontario Human Rights Commission finds this outdated and puts forward the term "racialized person" or "racialized group" to capture the social construction nature of race.[196] Race as a socially constructed hierarchical differentiation of people is an act of racialization, or "the process by which societies construct races as real, different and unequal in ways that matter to economic, political and social life."[197] For Zaman, this is interchangeably used with the term "racialized" people or communities or systemic marginalization of certain people groups.[198] This distinction of being a minority also means less influence and power due to such ethnic classification.

Another concern is the use of the term minority as visible minorities are not anymore minorities in some cities in Canada such as Richmond, BC, and Markham, Ontario, and the projection that minorities in Toronto, Vancouver, and Calgary will be majorities by 2036.[199] Yet, their majority in several areas do not reflect the general experience of marginality in the whole of Canadian society where there is still the predominance of Caucasian and people of European descent. The preponderance of racial and ethnic discrimination is an

---

[192] Statistics Canada, "Visible Minority of Person."

[193] Statistics Canada, "Visible Minority of Person."

[194] Statistics Canada, "Generation Status: Canadian-born Children of Immigrants," https://www12.statcan.gc.ca/nhs-enm/2011/as-sa/99-010-x/99-010-x2011003_2-eng.cfm.

[195] Michael Bach, "What's in a Name," *Canadian Centre for Diversity and Inclusion*, May 1, 2019, https://ccdi.ca/blog/what-s-in-a-name/.

[196] Ontario Human Rights Commission, "Racial Discrimination, Race and Racism (Fact Sheet)," n.d., https://www.ohrc.on.ca/en/racial-discrimination-race-and-racism-fact-sheet.

[197] Ontario Human Rights Commission, "Racial Discrimination, Race and Racism."

[198] Habiba Zaman, "Racialization and Marginalization of Immigrants: A New Wave of Xenophobia in Canada," *Labour/Le Travail* 66 (Fall 2010): 164.

[199] Tavia Grant and Denise Balkissoon, "'Visible Minority': Is It Time for Canada to Scrap the Term?," *The Globe and Mail*, February 6, 2019, https://www.theglobeandmail.com/canada/article-visible-minority-term-statscan/.

expression of the perpetual nature of marginality of diaspora visible minorities particularly in the season where immigration is at an all-time high. While immigration increases their numerical representation, the issue of institutional representation is still something to be desired.

There are concerns beyond Canada about the use of the term. The Committee on the Elimination of Racial Discrimination of the United Nations reported in 2007 regarding its concern of the use of "visible minorities" by the Canadian government in that it may not be "in accordance with the aims and objectives of the Convention".[200] The Convention refers to the International Convention on the Elimination of All Forms of Racial Discrimination. The Report claims that even if its original intent by the Canadian government is to address employment equity and, therefore, not used for the purpose of defining racial discrimination, "the term is widely used in official documents of the State party, including the Census."[201]

In this regard, the Convention states that racial discrimination shall mean any distinction, exclusion, restriction or preference based on race, colour, descent, or national or ethnic origin which has the purpose or effect of nullifying or impairing the recognition, enjoyment or exercise, on an equal footing, of human rights and fundamental freedoms in the political, economic, social, cultural or any other field of public life."[202] Thus, the term is seen in itself as discriminatory. Furthermore, the Committee on Elimination of Racial Discrimination of the United Nations is concerned with the term due to its homogenizing tendency and obscures the different experiences of minority groups.[203] The Committee further referred to a report of the Independent Expert on Minority Issues that conducted its mission to Canada in October 2009, which states that, "minority communities felt strongly that using a catch all terminology such as 'visible minority' had led to the neglect of specific

---

[200] United Nations, "Report of the Committee on the Elimination of Racial Discrimination, Seventy-First Session" (July 30- August 17, 2007): 17, https://www.un-ilibrary.org/content/books/9789210558549/read.

[201] United Nations, "Report of the Committee on the Elimination of Racial Discrimination," 17.

[202] United Nations, "International Convention on the Elimination of All Forms of Racial Discrimination," December 21, 1965, 2, https://www.ohchr.org/en/instruments-mechanisms/instruments/international-convention-elimination-all-forms-racial.

[203] United Nations, "Committee on Elimination of Racial Discrimination Considers Report of Canada," February 23, 2012, https://www.ungeneva.org/en/news-media/press/taxonomy/term/175/45070/committee-elimination-racial-discrimination-considers.

identifies and situations and obscured the distinct experiences of minority groups."[204]

As of 2021 Census, Statistics Canada has adopted the term "racialized groups" in analyzing information but uses visible minority categories still. For this Census, "racialized groups are based on and measured using the detailed "visible minority" variable, in accordance with existing Statistics Canada standards."[205] At this stage, it is reviewing the concept and is holding the "Visible Minority Concept Consultative Engagement" to modernize its ethnic classification.[206]

A significant concern, however, goes beyond the issue of the status of minorities but of the conception of the term minority as similar to the way race was developed as a social construct. This is more profound when applied to the concept of ethnicity. The concept of ethnic minority is a social construction developed by those in the majority. Kallen delineated key issues in this social construction. Primarily, applying the term ethnic to only ethnic minorities is misleading as it is used to set them apart from the dominant population, and is thereby applied only to ethnicities other than the Anglo-Canadian community.[207] Furthermore, the distinction made on the ethnicity of minorities is seen as an imposition to 'inferiorize' these groups. Thus, Kallen adds:

> Minorities are not 'natural' entities; they are socially constructed categories of people. No human population is innately or 'naturally' superior or inferior to others. However, some populations have more power than others and those with superior power (majorities) are able to impose *inferiorizing* labels on those with less power on the basis of their own unsubstantiated assumptions about minority group attributes. Minorities are not 'inferior' by nature, in any of their group attributes, but they become 'inferiorized' by majority definition.[208]

Every attempt to categorize minorities always has an element of marginality as it is mostly developed by the dominant culture. It is for this reason that Statistics Canada seeks to find meaningful categories that do not have elements of discrimination and recognize the struggles and challenges of minority communities.

---

[204] United Nations, "Committee on Elimination of Racial Discrimination Considers Report of Canada."
[205] Statistics Canada, "The Canadian Census: A Rich Portrait of the Country's Religious and Ethnocultural Diversity," October 26, 2022, https://www150.statcan.gc.ca/n1/daily-quotidien/221026/dq221026b-eng.htm.
[206] Statistics Canada, "The Canadian Census."
[207] Evelyn Kallen, *Ethnicity and Human Rights in Canada*, Third Edition (Ontario, Canada: Oxford University Press, 2003), 75.
[208] Kallen, "Ethnicity and Human Rights in Canada," 75.

Race and Ethnicity

It is imperative at this stage to make further distinction between race and ethnicity. Race and ethnicity are two different terms. Bryce noted that this has been sloppily used interchangeably.[209] There is a common understanding though of how the two terms are to be understood as distinct categorization of people. Race is understood as categorization of people based on physical traits while ethnicity is a distinction based on cultural expression. Thus, "race is often perceived as something that's inherent in our biology, and therefore inherited across generations. Ethnicity, on the other hand, is typically understood as something we acquire, or self-ascribe, based on factors like where we live or the culture we share with others."[210] There is a common understanding then that race is used to categorize people based on biological traits while ethnicity defines cultural identity. Morin delineates that the way race is defined as a physical characteristic is commonly based on hair texture and skin color.[211] There is definite research, however, proving that skin color has nothing to do with biological differences and is no more than a purely environmental adaptive mechanism.[212] Furthermore, there is broad perspective that race is a social construction and was developed only in the 18th century to cement permanent consideration of groups as either superior or inferior.[213] There is, thus, a hierarchical element to race. In the current setting, there is still a tendency to interchange the two terms. This is seen in how racism and racial discrimination is defined. Racism is defined as "a belief that humans can be divided into a hierarchy of power on the basis of their differences in race and ethnicity. With some groups seen as superior to others on the sole basis of their racial or ethnic characteristics."[214] Racial discrimination is also defined as inclusive of ethnicity and is delineated as unfavorable treatment of others or

---

[209] Emma Bryce and Stephanie Pappas, "What's the Difference between Race and Ethnicity?," *Livescience.Com*, November 3, 2022, https://www.livescience.com/difference-between-race-ethnicity.html.

[210] Bryce and Pappas, What's the Difference between Race and Ethnicity.".

[211] Amy Morin, "What's the Difference Between Race and Ethnicity?," *Verywell Mind*, October 19, 2022, https://www.verywellmind.com/difference-between-race-and-ethnicity-5074205.

[212] Nina G. Jablonski and George Chaplin, "Human Skin Pigmentation as an Adaptation to UV Radiation," *Proceedings of the National Academy of Sciences* 107, no. supplement_2 (May 5, 2010): 8962–68, https://doi.org/10.1073/pnas.0914628107.

[213] "Race," Britannica.com, n.d., https://www.britannica.com/topic/race-human/Scientific-classifications-of-race.

[214] J.S. Frideres, "Racism," *Tha Canadian Encyclopedia*, February 7, 2006, https://www.thecanadianencyclopedia.ca/en/article/racism.

"any discrimination against any individual on the basis of their skin color, or racial or ethnic origin."[215]

There is a problem with the current interchange of race and ethnicity. Of specific concern is that race focuses on the negative nature of human identity and distinction. This is natural as it is a social construction developed to consider others as different and inferior. Ethnicity as a differentiator encompasses the whole gamut of biological, cultural, and social distinctions that provide value identity to people groups rather than a consideration of their superior or inferior status. Morin stated that ethnicity has a broader meaning than race as it is inclusive of "commonalities such as race, national origin, tribal heritage, religion, language, and culture can describe someone's ethnicity."[216]

This goes back to the biblical use of "*ethnos*" as a purveyor of God's desire for plurality. While race is currently equated with ethnicity, the conception of ethnicity as a marker of identity has significant bearing on diaspora visible minorities as their experience of marginality is not just on the matter of inferior status based on physical features but on their "otherness" from the dominant majority culture. Such otherness includes physical traits, language, and cultural practices.

In the biblical context, ethnic discrimination and marginalization are expressed through the maltreatment and oppression of foreigners, with foreigners being the identity of other ethnic groups who are distinct from Israel but chose to live within the Jewish society. It is this ethnic identity that denotes the foreigner status of diaspora visible minorities, leading to their experience and condition of marginality.

Rationale for Focus on the Concept of Visible Minority

This book will continue to use "visible minority" rather than "racialized group" due to the current review status where there is no clarity on terminology at this stage. It is to be noted that the definition of Statistics Canada as a descriptor provides both racial and ethnic categorization. In defining visible minorities as non-Caucasian, it already provides a racial categorization between the majority Caucasian people and the other non-Caucasian minorities. It is, thus, obvious that while the term is used as a neutral categorization, it could not be avoided to continue investigating the use of the term and that a better term is still needed.

In stating this, the value of the term visible minority is its categorization of non-Caucasian races in their different ethnic groups. In delineating specific ethnic groups under visible minorities, it provides the rationale for affirming

---

[215] Office of United Nations High Commissioner for Human Rights, "Racial Discrimination," *The United Nations*, https://www.ohchr.org/en/taxonomy/term/903.

[216] Morin, "What's the Difference between Race and Ethnicity."

the need to focus on the marginality of non-European groups. It is not the objective of the book to homogenize the experience of minority groups but to find common experiences among them. While there are differences in marginality experience, it is evident that such commonality exists. A study conducted in Australia, which has also significant diaspora population, revealed this commonality. The study sought to measure labor market discrimination across different minority groups in Australia, wherein one quarter of the population was born overseas. The racial and ethnic groups that were studied and comparison of experience sought were those of Anglo-Saxon, Italians, Chinese, Indigenous, and Middle Eastern backgrounds. The study revealed Anglos-Saxons and Italians experienced less discrimination compared to Chinese and Middle Eastern groups.[217]

The previous discussion on race as a social construct directs this research to focus on ethnicity as closer to the biblical construct of *ethnos*. The term "visible minority" captures both the distinct ethnic identities of diaspora groups and their status of marginality. There is then value in focusing on the broader ethnic categorization of people groups beyond physical or biological differences. This does not seek to negate the distinct experiences of different minority groups nor their racialization. It is beyond the scope of this research to determine specific and distinct experiences of racism and racial discrimination of diaspora communities in Canada. Furthermore, the book seeks to go beyond the issue of racialization of minority groups and attempts to determine the common condition of people groups that are culturally or ethnically different from the majority culture rather than as an attempt at homogenization of experiences.

Ethnic Composition of Diaspora Visible Minorities in Canada

Canada is a mosaic of ethnicities and cultures. As an affirmation of this diversity, Multiculturalism became an official policy by the Canadian government on October 8, 1971, and passed into law through the Canadian Multiculturalism Act in 1988.[218] This is also affirmed in section 27 of the Canadian Charter of Rights and Freedom. Of the total population of

---

[217] Alison Booth, Andrew Leigh, and Elena Varganova, "Does Racial and Ethnic Discrimination Vary across Minority Groups? Evidence from a Field Experiment," *IZA Discussion Papers*, May 2010.

[218] David Berry, "Canadian Multiculturalism Act," *The Canadian Encyclopedia*, March 25, 2020, https://www.thecanadianencyclopedia.ca/en/article/canadian-multiculturalism-act.

36,991,981,[219] more than 450 ethnic or cultural origins were reported in the 2021 Census.[220]

Canada is a nation that is highly dependent on immigration for its economic growth. Its immigration policy is skewed towards admitting immigrants under the economic category. In the 2016 census, 6 in 10 immigrants are under the economic category.[221] The same census shows that more than 1 in 5 Canadians are foreign-born. Furthermore, between 2011 to 2016, 61.8% of immigrants were born in Asia. This trend continued as expressed in the 2021 Census. In 2021 alone, Canada brought in 406,000 permanent residents which are the most immigrants in a single year in its history.[222] This will further increase with Canada's Immigration Level Plan aiming to welcome 465,000 new permanent residents in 2023, 485,000 in 2024 and 500,000 in 2025.[223]

Yet even with the increasing immigration trends, the current demographics in the country still show the predominance of people of European background. Furthermore, close to 70% of the population or over 25 million reported being White.[224] The 2021 Census revealed that 1.5 million people reported their origin as Canadian or 15% of the population. The topmost origins are also of European background with 5.3 million reporting English background, 4.4 million Irish, 4.4 million Scottish, and 4 million French.[225] Approximately 2.2 million reported indigenous ancestry.[226] The Census revealed that 52.2% of the population reported European origins. The 2021 Census further revealed that 1.7 million reported Chinese as their origin, 1.3 million that are of Indian origin, and 0.9 million of Filipino origin.[227]

The immigration trend shown in the 2016 Census that revealed most immigrants coming from Asia is reflected in the 2021 Census. From 2016 to

---

[219] Statistics Canada, "2021 Census of Population," February 9, 2022, https://www12.statcan.gc.ca/census-recensement/2021/dp-pd/prof/index.cfm?Lang=E.

[220] Statistics Canada, "The Canadian Census."

[221] Statistics Canada, "Immigration and Ethnocultural Diversity: Key Results from the 2016 Census," October 25, 2017, https://www150.statcan.gc.ca/n1/daily-quotidien/171025/dq171025b-eng.htm?indid=14428-1&indgeo=0.

[222] Immigration, Refugees and Citizenship Canada, "2022 Annual Report to Parliament on Immigration," December 21, 2022, https://www.canada.ca/en/immigration-refugees-citizenship/corporate/publications-manuals/annual-report-parliament-immigration-2022.html.

[223] "Notice – Supplementary Information for the 2023-2025 Immigration Levels Plan," November 1, 2022, https://www.canada.ca/en/immigration-refugees-citizenship/news/notices/supplementary-immigration-levels-2023-2025.html.

[224] Statistics Canada, "The Canadian Census."

[225] Statistics Canada, "The Canadian Census."

[226] Statistics Canada, "The Canadian Census."

[227] Statistics Canada, "The Canadian Census."

2021, Asia (including the Middle East) account for 62% of immigrants. India took the top spot as the primary place of birth of new immigrants to Canada (18.6%), followed by the Philippines (11.4% and China (8.9%).[228]

As mentioned earlier, the 2021 Census utilized racialized groups instead of visible minorities in view of the ongoing review and investigation of the latter concept in categorizing minorities and people of non-European background. As stated, while using the term racialized group, racialized group measurement still uses visible minority variables.[229] In this regard, the 2021 Census considers both racial and ethnic profiles in its categorization of people groups. Thus, the categorization of racialized groups is reflective of the previous delineation of visible minorities: South Asian, Chinese, Black, Filipino, Arab, Latin American, Southeast Asian, West Asian, Korean and Japanese. The Census revealed that 1 in 4 people are part of a racialized group or visible minority.

Table 5. Population of Visible Minorities

Population Group	Number (in millions)	Percentage
South Asians	2.6	7.1
Chinese	1.7	4.7
Black	1.5	4.3
Filipinos	.960	2.6
Arabs	.690	1.9
Latin Americans	.580	1.6
Southeast Asians	.390	1.1
West Asians	.360	1.0
Koreans	.220	0.6
Japanese	.099	0.3

Source: Statistics Canada, "The Canadian Census: A Rich Portrait of the Country's Religious and Ethnocultural Diversity," October 26, 2022, https://www150.statcan.gc.ca/n1/daily-quotidien/221026/dq221026b-eng.htm.

The visible minority population continues to grow with immigration as the main driver of this growth. Visible minorities or racialized groups account for 69.3% of the immigrant population and 83.0% for recent immigrants.[230] These groupings of visible minorities does not fully capture the ethnic diversity of the minority population. The largest visible minority groups (South Asians, Chinese, and Black) could be further categorized into different ethnic origins,

---

[228] Statistics Canada, "Immigrants Make up the Largest Share of the Population in over 150 Years and Continue to Shape Who We Are as Canadians," October 26, 2022, https://www150.statcan.gc.ca/n1/daily-quotidien/221026/dq221026a-eng.htm.
[229] Statistics Canada, "The Canadian Census."
[230] Statistics Canada, "The Canadian Census."

and linguistic and religious diversities. As to the latter, immigration by visible minorities significantly increased religious diversity. Although more than one in three Canadians reported having no religious affiliation, the increasing number of people from South Asia led to increase of people reporting Muslim, Hindu, and Sikh backgrounds and have doubled in the last 20 years.[231] A previous study by the Pew Research Center bears this out that showed that in 2011, 11% of the population identify themselves as Muslim, Sikh, Hindu, Buddhist, Jewish, or an adherent of other religions.[232]

Even with the increasing trend of people reporting these religious affiliations from diaspora visible minorities, there are nuances to this religious makeup. There is a significant shift happening in Canadian society on religious makeup that is also happening among diaspora visible minorities in relation to the people reporting not having any religious affiliation due to religious switching. A study in 2017 concluded that "the patterns of religious switching of immigrants present similarities with that of the Canadian-born even if, in relative terms, net population change associated with religious switching is of a lower magnitude among the immigrant population in the most recent period."[233] There is a pervading pattern among all Canadian born populations that the younger generation is more likely to report no religious affiliation. Thus, "in general, the younger the cohort, the lower the proportion of those who reported having a religious affiliation, the less frequent the participation in group religious activities, the less frequent the individual religious or spiritual activities, and the less importance given to religious and spiritual beliefs in how one lives one's life."[234] A study by the Pew Research Center explained that this phenomenon is due to generational replacement, with the older generation who are mostly religiously active being supplanted by the newer generation.[235]

The status of Christianity also saw a shift in number. The 2021 Census revealed that "more than 19.3 million people reported a Christian religion, or just over half of the Canadian population (53.3%). However, this percentage is down from 67.3% in 2011 and 77.1% in 2001."[236] These social and cultural

---

[231] Statistics Canada, "The Canadian Census."
[232] Pew Research Center, "Canada's Changing Religious Landscape," *Pew Research Center's Religion & Public Life Project*, June 27, 2013, https://www.pewforum.org/2013/06/27/canadas-changing-religious-landscape/.
[233] Éric Caron-Malenfant, Anne Goujon, and Vegard Skirbekk, "The Religious Switching of Immigrants in Canada," *Journal of Ethnic and Migration Studies* 44, no. 15 (November 17, 2017): 2582–2602.
[234] Louis Cornelissen, "Religiosity in Canada and Its Evolution from 1985 to 2019," *Statistics Canada*, October 28, 2021, https://www150.statcan.gc.ca/n1/pub/75-006-x/2021001/article/00010-eng.htm.
[235] Pew Research Center, "Canada's Changing Religious Landscape."
[236] Statistics Canada, "The Canadian Census."

changes are more impactful in the religious climate of the country which gradually saw the decline of Christianity's influence in Canadian society. An analysis by the Pew Research Center's Forum on Religion and Public Life of the Canada Census (1971-2001) and National Household Survey (2011) confirmed this decline with a drop in the percentage of Canadians who identified themselves as Catholics and Protestants.[237] The study revealed that, from the period of 1971 to 2011, there is a drop from 43% to 39% among those who identified themselves as Catholics, and a steep drop from 41% to 27% among Protestants.

How does Christian diaspora visible minorities impact religion, church life, and mission in Canada though? While there is manifested religious switching among the younger second-generation immigrants, attendance to religious activities is still higher among these group of immigrants than the general population where 43% reported religious attendance at least once a month, in contrast to only 22% among native-born.[238] Of particular consideration on the impact of immigration is that immigrants are also filling the pews of Christian churches. Anecdotal evidence that reverberates in other provinces and cities in the country captures this change:

> James Paton, a pastor at Calgary's First Alliance Church, noted that his church has seen significant growth in numbers of visible minorities, including new immigrants to the country. "We have a lot of people from China, the Philippines, Iran, Iraq, and Latin America," he said, and the church now provides translation services into Spanish, Mandarin, and Farsi.[239]

This change will further reshape the makeup of Canadian churches, not only in terms of the representation but also doctrinal posture. In the light of the increasing liberalism of mainline denominations, immigrants will be a significant force in reviving Evangelicalism. John Stackhouse stated that as the current migration trend is from the Pacific Rim, the influx of Chinese and Korean Christians is reshaping evangelicalism towards a more conservative and pietistic form.[240]

---

[237] Pew Research Center, "Canada's Changing Religious Landscape."
[238] Pew Research Center, "Canada's Changing Religious Landscape."
[239] Xiao Xu, "Immigrants Providing a Boost to Declining Church Attendance in Canada," *The Globe and Mail*, December 22, 2017, https://www.theglobeandmail.com/news/british-columbia/immigrants-providing-a-boost-to-declining-church-attendance-in-canada/article37423409/.
[240] John G. Stackhouse Jr., "The Rise and Fall (and Rise?) Of Evangelicalism in Canada," *The Evangelical Fellowship of Canada*, September 11, 2017, https://www.evangelicalfellowship.ca/Communications/Articles/September-2017/The-rise-and-fall-(and-rise-)-of-evangelicalism-in.

The current immigration policy of the Canadian government will further cement the increasing number of diaspora visible minorities. This will significantly change the population demographics with the possibility of the minority becoming the majority in the near future. Two cities in the country—Richmond, BC, and Markham, Ontario—now have visible minorities as the majority. Statistics Canada expressed that if the trend continues, immigrants could represent 34% of the population.[241] The immigration trend is also shifting the population movement in the country as immigrants are settling outside key urban centers (Toronto, Vancouver, and Montreal) and towards small urban areas where they have existing social networks, economic and employment opportunities, and finding the general appeal of the area.[242]

These immigration trend where visible minorities are shifting Canadian demographics has significant missiological implications and will continue to reshape the face of Canadian churches. What is of concern though is its implications for their experience of marginality.

History of Marginality of Diaspora Visible Minorities in Canada

Marginality as an issue for diaspora visible minorities is not a new phenomenon and is rooted in the political dynamics and immigration policies throughout Canada's history. Thus, Satzewich and Liodakis stated that "in Canada, many of the issues and struggles that ethnic groups and Aboriginal peoples face today are rooted in the political and economic decisions, individual actions, and government policies and practices many years ago."[243] Peeling further into history, the formation of the nation through colonization carries with it the existing mentality of the European colonizers who have been steeped in the idea of race developed in the eighteenth century. There is a pervading perspective that racism and ethnocentrism are already imbedded in the act of colonization through the belief that Aboriginal peoples are non-Christian and have not been organized into states, and therefore can benefit from "the guidance of a superior people."[244]

Satzewich and Liodakis clarified, however, that while there may be an element of racism in this colonial endeavor, it has to be seen in the broader context of colonial expansion and state formation, both for the French and the British settlers. With the British dominating power in Canada in 1763 through the Royal Proclamation, their entering into land surrender treaties with the original inhabitants was to "provide a legal basis for settlement, economic

---

[241] Statistics Canada, "Immigrants Make up the Largest Share of the Population."
[242] Statistics Canada, "Immigrants Make up the Largest Share of the Population."
[243] Vic Satzewich and Nikolaos Liodakis, *'Race' And Ethnicity in Canada: A Critical Introduction* (Ontario, Canada: Oxford University Press, 2007), 29.
[244] Satzewich and Liodakis, *'Race' and Ethnicity in Canada*, 34.

expansion, and the eventual formation of the Canadian nation."[245] It must be noted that colonial powers, including the French and English, claim their right to indigenous lands through the Doctrine of Discovery. The Doctrine is based on the declarations of several Popes in the 15th century. "These declarations (known as "papal bulls") provided religious authority for Christian empires to invade and subjugate non-Christian lands, peoples and sovereign nations, impose Christianity on these populations, and claim their resources."[246] Interestingly, the Canadian government still continues to use the Doctrine as legal bases to claim unceded indigenous lands.[247]

While this thrust towards state formation is delineated in the context of the Aboriginal peoples, this is also applied in Canada's immigration policy to bring in settlers from different nations to strengthen the new nation's economic development from its founding until the present. State formation does not absolve, however, the inherent and subsequent racism, discrimination, and social inequalities experienced by Aboriginal peoples through the actions and policies of the French and British colonialists and are reflected later in the experiences of new immigrants.[248] These experiences of immigrants, however, vary depending on their racial and ethnic backgrounds.

It is not possible to deal with Canadian state formation and immigration without considering the impact on indigenous communities. While the visible minorities experience marginality, nowhere is this more pronounced than in the experience of the First Nations who have been impacted and forced out of their land due to the state formation purposes of the government and their experience of marginalization up to the present. This requires, however, in-depth research which could not be fully covered in this book.

Immigration as a policy for economic development strengthened in the 19th century. Societal responses and reactions to immigration varied with groups opposed to open-door Immigration Policy.[249] English-speaking Canadians were concerned about desirability of immigrants while French- speaking Canadians were worried about the status of French Canada within Confederation.[250] Racial categories were used as basis of desirability. "British and American immigrants were regarded as the most desirable, followed by northern and western Europeans, central and eastern Europeans and then by Jews and southern

---

[245] Satzewich and Liodakis, *'Race' and Ethnicity in Canada*, 35–36.

[246] Travis Tomchuk, "The Doctrine of Discovery," *Canadian Museum for Human Rights*, November 2, 2022, https://humanrights.ca/story/doctrine-discovery.

[247] Tomchuk, "The Doctrine of Discovery."

[248] See chapters 4 and 6, Satzewich and Liodakis, *'Race' and Ethnicity in Canada*.

[249] Howard Palmer and Leo Driedger, "Prejudice and Discrimination in Canada," *The Canadian Encyclopedia*, February 10, 2011, https://www.thecanadianencyclopedia.ca/en/article/prejudice-and-discrimination.

[250] Palmer and Driedger, "Prejudice and Discrimination in Canada."

Europeans. Close to the bottom of the pecking order were the pacifist religious sects, such as the German-speaking Hutterites and Mennonites, and the Russian-speaking Doukhobors."[251]

Immigration process in Canada in its formative years was based on social desirability. To quote at length:

> The first 60 years of the twentieth century saw sustained efforts by the government to control immigration of people who were defined as unsuitable because of their 'race', ethnicity, or country of origin. The social evaluation of immigrants was based on a racialized hierarchy of desirability in which some groups were seen s both good workers and desirable future citizens and should be encouraged to come; some were regarded as 'racially' unsuitable for life in Canada and should be prevented from coming; and some were 'in-between' people who, while perhaps posing certain long and short-term problems for Canada, could be admitted as a last resort.[252]

In this process, non-Europeans and non-White groups were considered at the "end of the social desirability" scale.[253] In particular, the Black community was the first immigrant group to be put on the bottom of the scale. Slavery was part of Canada during colonial times and during its nation-building period. As early as the 1600s, in the French colony (New France), slavery was a common practice.[254] Even with the British abolition of slavery in 1807, and in spite of the fact that many Canadians were against slavery, Blacks were treated as source of cheap labor.[255] Together with the Black community, Asian immigrants (Chinese, Japanese, and South Asians) "were considered inferior and unable to be assimilated into Canadian society."[256]

There are distinct historical timelines that are significant points of reference on the experience of discrimination, racism, and marginality of diaspora visible minorities. Among the Asian immigrants the Chinese became the first subject of significant discrimination. The Chinese diaspora started in 1788 when Captain John Meares brought 50 Chinese to build a trading post in Nootka Sound, British Columbia.[257] The Chinese community grew with the arrival of gold

---

[251] Palmer and Driedger, "Prejudice and Discrimination in Canada."
[252] Satzewich and Liodakis, *'Race' and Ethnicity in Canada*, 45.
[253] Satzewich and Liodakis, *'Race' and Ethnicity in Canada*, 48.
[254] Matthew McRae and Steve McCullough, "The Story of Black Slavery in Canadian History," *Canadian Museum for Human Rights*, August 22, 2018, https://humanrights.ca/story/story-black-slavery-canadian-history.
[255] Palmer and Driedger, "Prejudice and Discrimination in Canada."
[256] Palmer and Driedger, "Prejudice and Discrimination in Canada."
[257] Government of Canada, "Significant Events in History of Canadians of Asian Heritage," April 29, 2021, https://www.canada.ca/en/canadian-heritage/campaigns/asian-heritage-month/important-events.html.

prospectors from San Francisco. A significant increase occurred, however, when Chinese workers were brought to Canada to build the Canadian Pacific Railway. Between 1881 and 1884, over 17,000 Chinese immigrants came as workers for the railway system.[258] The reason for the focus on Chinese immigrants at this stage is that their increasing number led to substantial political and social backlash. In 1885, the Chinese Immigration Act was established to impose a duty of $50 on every Chinese person to enter Canada. Known as the Head Tax, this legislation is considered as the first Canadian legislation to "exclude immigrants on the basis of their ethnic origin."[259] The Head Tax was further increased to $100 in 1900 and $500 in 1903. The Electoral Franchise Act of 1885 also prohibited immigrants of Chinese origin to vote in Federal elections.[260] The Head Tax was only partly able to stem Chinese entry and so in 1923, Canadian Parliament passed the Chinese Immigration Act of 1923, or the Chinese Exclusion Act, that further limited Chinese immigration by limiting categories of immigrants and prevented family reunification.[261]

The other Asian groups affected by exclusionary policies and discrimination were the Japanese and South Asians. In fact, there was a strong anti-Asian sentiment particularly in British Columbia and other provinces with anti-Asian riots taking place as well as outright discrimination including exclusion from public schools, having no right to vote, exclusion from gaining employment in public offices, and other forms of social discrimination. One significant event that took place was the Komagata Maru incident. In May 23, 1914, a boat named Komagata Maru carrying 376 prospective South Asian immigrants was prevented from docking in Vancouver due to fierce public opposition. Prior to this, the government placed restrictions on South Asian immigration by requiring "Asiatic" immigrants to possess $200 to enter the country.[262] A second requirement forced immigrants to come to Canada via a "continuous journey" from the country of origin.[263] The Komagata Maru was chartered by the Sikh

---

[258] Government of Canada, "Significant Events in History of Canadians of Asian Heritage."

[259] Daniel Meister et al., "The Chinese Immigration Act, 1885," *Canadian Museum of Immigration at Pier 21*, n.d., https://pier21.ca/research/immigration-history/the-chinese-immigration-act-1885. See also, Ninette Kelley and Michael Trebilcock, *The Making of the Mosaic: A History of Canadian Immigration Policy* (Toronto: University of Toronto Press, 1998), 107.

[260] Government of Canada, "Significant Events in History of Canadians of Asian Heritage."

[261] Government of Canada, "Significant Events in History of Canadians of Asian Heritage."

[262] Government of Canada, "The Komagata Maru Incident of 1914," https://www.canada.ca/en/parks-canada/news/2016/08/the-komagata-maru-incident-of-1914.html.

[263] Government of Canada, "The Komagata Maru Incident of 1914."

businessman Gurdit Singh as an attempt to challenge this restriction by chartering a boat from Hong Kong.[264] In spite of the legal defense of the local South Asian community, the boat was prevented from docking, causing the passengers to suffer from lack of access to water and food. The boat was forced to return to India after a month.

Right up to the second world war, there was outright racism and social discrimination against non-white immigrants. Even before the second world war, there were already hostilities against Japanese immigration and existing Japanese immigrants. These include the "Gentlemen's Agreement" between Canada and Japan to limit Japanese immigration, limiting licenses to Japanese fishermen, and laws preventing White women to work in Chinese and Japanese-owned businesses.[265] The first and second world wars brought their own forms of discrimination against all immigrants, including those with European backgrounds who were identified with enemy countries. The lessening of opposition to non-white immigration and tolerance to immigrants came about only in the 1950's and 1960's with the passing of provincial rights bills and the institution of the Canadian Bill of Rights.

The 1960's was a watershed moment for the political, cultural, and social climate of Canada. All over the country, cultural and social changes took place that saw the decline of the influence of traditional institutions through political changes and liberalization laws. Immigration policies became more open and second and third generation immigrants gained socio-economic mobility. Subsequent immigration acts were geared towards bolstering economic development and immigration was seen as an engine for this growth. The thrust towards social equity went together with this development. It was obvious that in the 1970's, the immigration inflow shifted from people of European descent to Asians.

The shift in societal values came into force in 1982 when the Canadian Charter of Rights and Freedoms was imbedded into the Canadian Constitution. The recognition of the values and equality of non-white diaspora communities was recognized with the provision that the charter "explicitly prohibits discrimination on the basis of colour, religion, sex, age, and physical or mental disability. It affirms linguistic rights and pre-existing Indigenous and treaty rights."[266] The recognition of the contribution of non-White immigrants was further bolstered with the institution of the Employment Equity Acts in 1986 which for the first time used the concept of Visible Minorities to refer to non-White diaspora communities.

---

[264] Government of Canada, "The Komagata Maru Incident of 1914."
[265] Palmer and Driedger, "Prejudice and Discrimination in Canada."
[266] Armando Perla, "The Canadian Charter of Rights and Freedoms," *Canadian Museum for Human Rights*, April 12, 2017, https://humanrights.ca/story/canadian-charter-rights-and-freedoms.

Yet prior to the institution of the Canadian Charter of Rights and Freedoms and the Employment Equity Act, the Canadian government has avowed multiculturalism as a government policy since October 8, 1971, in recognition of the increasing immigration from non-European countries and gradual change in ethnicity of the Canadian population. Multiculturalism was also imbedded in section 27 of the Charter of Rights and Freedoms. This policy is, however, just a recognition of diversity rather than creating substantive change in policy.[267] Of further concern is that "though it was official policy, the government's support of multiculturalism was criticized for being largely symbolic. Few resources were devoted to the initiative, and critics suggested it was more concerned with promoting identity than addressing concerns about equitable treatment in Canadian society."[268] Due to such limitations, and to put teeth to the policy, the policy was established as a law through the Multiculturalism Act on July 21, 1988. As a law, the government seeks to "recognize and promote the understanding that multiculturalism reflects the cultural and racial diversity of Canadian society and acknowledges the freedom of all members of Canadian society to preserve, enhance and share their cultural heritage," and, "promote the full and equitable participation of individuals and communities of all origins in the continuing evolution and shaping of all aspects of Canadian society and assist them in the elimination of any barrier to that participation."[269]

The historical trends shaping marginalization of visible minorities and the governmental policy on multiculturalism need to be reflected also in the church formation in the country. The issue of exclusion could also be found in church formation. Lau expressed that "majority of mainstream evangelical churches are still primarily monocultural congregations, segregated by ethno-historical culture and denominational doctrine."[270] This then compels diaspora churches to gather among themselves due to such lack of welcome and integration. The Canadian government's multicultural policies could even be factors in further marginalization. Lau's study on the influence of multiculturalism on ethnic diversity in Evangelical churches expressed that this had not really been helpful in intercultural church formation as he surmised that "the values of Canadian

---

[267] Daniel Meister et al., "Canadian Multiculturalism Policy, 1971," n.d., https://pier21.ca/research/immigration-history/canadian-multiculturalism-policy-1971.
[268] Berry, "Canadian Multiculturalism Act."
[269] Government of Canada, "Canadian Multiculturalism Act," July 1, 1988, https://laws-lois.justice.gc.ca/eng/acts/c-18.7/page-1.html.
[270] Sherman Lau, "Is Multiculturalism 'Bad' for the Church?," *Mission Central*, October 4, 2019, https://www.missioncentral.ca/posts/2019/10/is-multiculturalism-bad-for-the-church.

multiculturalism, i.e., accommodation, tolerance, and coexistence, are contrary to achieving a Kingdom-inspired intercultural community."[271]

Nature of Marginality of Diaspora Visible Minorities in Canada

The establishment of policies and laws to negate exclusion and discrimination of diaspora visible minorities has significantly reduced the barriers that they face in integration in Canadian society. The changing demographics due to immigration has also substantially altered the social dynamics with visible minorities becoming majorities in some major cities. While this might be the case, there are still significant barriers in the present that diaspora visible minorities face and are affecting their integration. Each ethnic group faces different conditions of marginality. As stated earlier, it is for this reason that the term *visible minority* is under review as it does not fully capture the differences in experiences and conditions of each of the minority communities.

Furthermore, the use of the term 'visible minority,' as applied to these ethnicities is already an act of marginalization where non-white or non-Caucasian backgrounds are lumped outside of the majority culture and are thereby distinct. This is interchangeably used with the term *racialized* people or communities or systemic marginalization of certain people groups.[272] This distinction of being a minority also means less influence and power due to such ethnic classification.

The state of marginality of immigrants is not only a matter of identity but also of experience. Thus, Gorospe defines marginalization as both a matter of social and structural invisibility and the experience of subaltern existence.[273] Subaltern means being in the lower social class, of being the other.[274] Gorospe claims that "the pain of marginality is made acute by being regarded as mere instruments of policy and by being subjected to ethnic, economic, and social differentiation."[275] This marginality is reflected in the Canadian context. This delineation of marginality does not present individual diaspora community experience but more of general findings that majority of all visible

---

[271] Sherman Lau, "The Influence of Canadian Multiculturalism on Ethnic Diversity in Evangelical Churches in Vancouver, British Columbia" (DIS Dissertation, Western Seminary, 2022), 26.

[272] Habiba Zaman, "Racialization and Marginalization of Immigrants: A New Wave of Xenophobia in Canada," *Labour/Le Travail* 66 (Fall 2010): 164.

[273] Athena Gorospe, "Case Study: Overseas Filipino Workers," *Evangelical Review of Theology* 31, no. 4 (October 2007): 370.

[274] See, Vinayak Chaturvedi, "A Critical Theory of Subalternity: Rethinking Class in Indian Historiography," *Left History: An Interdisciplinary Journal of Historical Inquiry and Debate* 12, no. 1 (Spring/Summer 2007), https://lh.journals.yorku.ca/index.php/lh/article/view/15042.

[275] Gorospe, "Case Study: Overseas Filipino Workers," 370.

minorities experience. Some groups will be highlighted as well to provide specific information about their condition.

Education and Labor Market Participation

Education and labor market participation is one of the key areas of concern for diaspora visible minorities. There is a plethora of anecdotal evidence of marginality ranging from non-acceptance of educational qualifications and credentials to discrimination in the labor market due to foreign sounding or non-western names. Labour force participation is "the total labour force (comprised of those who are employed and unemployed, combined) relative to the size of the working-age population. In other words, it is the share of the working-age population that is working or looking for work."[276] Employment and labour force participation are key indicators of how visible minorities fare in Canadian society for this reflects income equality or inequality. A study by Block and Galabuzi of the 2006 Census already showed marginality in the area of labour and revealed the "racialization of poverty" in Canada which is linked to low-income jobs.[277] The study showed that in that period, while the majority of visible minorities have higher labour force participation rate than non-visible minorities, specific ethnicities (Japanese, Chinese, Korean or Arab/West Asian), have lower labour force participation than non-visible minorities. Of specific concern as well is that, except for Japanese and Filipinos, the rest of the visible minorities experience higher unemployment rates, or 2.4% higher than non-racialized Canadians.[278] Furthermore, "the unemployment rate for those who identify as Chinese was 21% higher than non-racialized Canadians. The unemployment rate was 95% higher for those who identify as West Asian/Arab and 73% higher for those who identify as Black."[279] Such trend continues as expressed in the 2021 Census, with some ethnicities experiencing the same employment condition. Table 9 shows that visible minorities have a higher labour participation rate of 67.9% compared to 62.2% for non-visible minorities.

---

[276] Statistics Canada, "Participation Rates," November 30, 2015, https://www150.statcan.gc.ca/n1/pub/71-222-x/2008001/sectiona/a-participation-activite-eng.htm.

[277] Sheila Block and Grace-Edward Galabuzi, "Canada's Colour Coded Labour Market," *Canadian Centre for Policy Alternatives and The Wellesley Institute*, March 2011, 5.

[278] Block and Galabuzi, "Canada's Colour Coded Labour Market," 7.

[279] Block and Galabuzi, "Canada's Colour Coded Labour Market," 7.

Table 6. Canada Visible Minorities Labor Force Participation, Employment Rate, Unemployment Rate 2021

Population Groups	Participation Rate	Employment Rate	Unemployment Rate
Total	63.7	57.1	10.3
Total visible minority population	67.9	59.4	12.5
South Asian	70.6	62.3	11.7
Chinese	59.2	51.9	12.3
Black	69.9	59.9	14.3
Filipino	76.5	70.1	8.4
Arab	63.7	53.6	15.8
Latin American	72.9	64.2	11.9
Southeast Asian	66.3	56.7	14.5
West Asian	65.7	55.3	15.9
Korean	64.6	56.6	12.5
Japanese	62.5	56.1	10.2
Visible minority (n.i.e)	66.6	57.3	13.9
Multiple visible minorities	68.3	58.5	14.4
Not a visible minority	62.2	56.3	9.5

Source: Statistics Canada. Table 98-10-0446-01 Labour force status by visible minority, immigrant status and period of immigration, highest level of education, age and gender: Canada, provinces and territories, census metropolitan areas and census agglomerations with parts. **DOI:** https://doi.org/10.25318/9810044601-eng

Visible minorities also have slightly higher employment rate of 59.4% compared to 56.3% for non-visible minorities, except for the Chinese, Arabs, West Asians, and Japanese. What is troubling however, is that visible minorities have a significantly higher unemployment rate of 12.5% compared to only 9.5% for non-visible minorities. Of all visible minorities, only Filipinos have lower unemployment rate (8.4%) than non-visible minorities.

The COVID-19 pandemic has further aggravated the situation of visible minorities, with all groups citing problems with meeting financial or essential needs compared to the non-visible minority population. A significant number of visible minority groups who have reported higher impact of the pandemic also cited having accessed income support to meet these financial obligations compared to the non-visible minority population.

Table 7. Pre-COVID-19 Job Loss, COVID-19 Impact on Financial Obligations, and Income Support Among Visible Minorities

Population Group	Experienced job loss or reduced hours among individuals employed before COVID-19	Reporting strong or moderate impact of COVID-19 on ability to meet financial obligations or essential needs	Applied and received federal income support among individuals reporting strong or moderate impact of COVID-19
South Asian	36.7	38.5	50.8
Chinese	31.2	26.8	49.5
Black	37.9	38.5	54.5
Filipino	42.2	42.9	64.5
Latin American	34.0	31.7	63.5
Arab	32.7	44.0	52.6
Southeast Asian	40.2	40.3	54.7
West Asian	46.5	42.0	61.1
Korean	40.1	36.1	67.7
Japanese	34.5	25.3	50.7
Others	36.6	33.1	55.3
White	34.1	23.2	45.7

Source: Statistics Canada, "Impacts of COVID-19 on Canadians - Trust in Others: Data Collection Series (5323)," as cited in, **Statistics Canada, "Impacts of COVID-19 on Immigrants and People Designated as Visible Minorities,"** October 20, 2020, https://www150.statcan.gc.ca/n1/pub/11-631-x/2020004/s6-eng.htm.

These statistics are further bolstered by studies on the relationship between education and employment. A case study of the Filipino community that is reflective of the overall immigrant population bears this out:

Filipinos' high educational levels seem to offer them little advantage in an increasingly polarized labor market.[280]

High educational attainment is often not recognized by Canadian employers and professional associations. As a result, Filipinos struggle to regain their professional status in Canada, and their story is one of income disparity.[281]

Increasingly, they have trouble working in their professions and end up working in manufacturing, food preparation, and retail jobs; in some cases, they never return to their field of training. The fact that this particular group is experiencing these problems, despite their English proficiency and high education levels, indicates the pervasiveness of these issues in Canada's immigrant population.[282]

One classic example is the lower categorization of Filipino immigrants who come under the Live-in Caregiver Program. A study by Pratt showed that placement agencies qualify European caregivers as professionals while Filipino caregivers as servants.[283] In this regard, while Filipinos have high employment rate, the nature and quality of their work is not commensurate with their qualifications.

Such pervasiveness of the issue in Canada's immigrant population is also borne out by another study that revealed that skilled immigrants in Canada face a higher level of unemployment and lower wages than non-immigrants due to discrimination.[284] Furthermore, the predominance of favoritism for the White population is evidenced by discrimination against applicants with foreign experience and foreign names. Thus, even if visible minority groups have high labour participation rate, the nature of their work reveals significant gap in income with the non-visible minority population. Barriers are also present in organizations with most immigrants not recognized in their skillset as most

---

[280] Ren Thomas, "The Filipino Case: Insights into Choice and Resiliency among Immigrants in Toronto" (2011), 6–7, https://renthomas.ca/wp-content/uploads/2009/11/The-Filipino-Case-Insights-into-choice-and-resiliency-among-immigrants-in-Toronto.pdf.
[281] Thomas, "The Filipino Case," 7.
[282] Thomas, "The Filipino Case," 17.
[283] Geraldine Pratt, "From Registered Nurse to Registered Nanny: Discursive Geographies of Filipina Domestic Workers in Vancouver, B.C.," *Economic Geography* 75, no. 3 (1999): 215–236, https://www.jstor.org/stable/144575.
[284] Philip Oreopoulos, "Why Do Skilled Immigrants Struggle in the Labor Market? A Field Experiment with Thirteen Thousand Resumes," *American Economic Journal: Economic Policy* 3, no. 4 (2011): 148–71.

Canadian organizations and companies don't consider putting immigrants in management or executive-level positions.[285]

Health Access

Aside from labor issues, health access and outcomes is one area of marginality for diaspora visible minorities. Clearly, health access is also influenced by race and ethnicity. A study on the impact of discrimination among minority immigrants in health services revealed evidence that discrimination is one of the key determinants of health. One study reviewed literature and research on such issue in other countries, as well as interviews done with health care providers and immigrant minorities in Ontario, Canada.[286] Of key concern that the study revealed is that immigrant minorities perceive that such discrimination happens at least once when interacting with health care providers.[287] Of further interest is that the study found out that such discrimination could either be interpersonal or systemic. In another study, there is race and ethnic disparities on health service access and health outcomes among ethnic populations.[288] What is specific about this study though is that it revealed that while there is no evidence the visible minorities having less access to general and specialist physicians and services, it's in the area of hospital utilization and cancer screening that they have lower utilization.[289] These studies affirm other studies worldwide on the intersectionality between ethnicity, race and health and further confirm racial and ethnic discrimination in health access by visible minorities. A broader country study by Waldron on the impact of inequality on health in Canada concluded that "in Canada, racialized, immigrant and refugee groups are most at risk for the negative health effects that result from persistent health disparities, arising from race, socio-economic status, poverty, citizenship status, and other social determinants, which expose them to macro-structural and micro-situational inequalities."[290]

---

[285] Sarah Dobson, "Skilled Immigrants Overlooked for Leadership Roles," *TRIEC*, April 25, 2016, https://triec.ca/skilled-immigrants-overlooked-for-leadership-roles/.

[286] Grace Pollock et al., "Perceptions of Discrimination in Health Services Experienced by Immigrant Minorities in Ontario," *Citizenship and Immigration Canada*, n.d..

[287] Pollock, et al., "Perceptions of Discrimination," 28.

[288] Hude Quan et al., "Variation in Health Services Utilization Among Ethnic Populations," *Canadian Medical Association Journal* 174, no. 6 (March 14, 2006): 787–91, https://doi.org/10.1503/cmaj.050674.

[289] Quan, et al., "Variation in Health Services."

[290] Ingrid RG Waldron, "The Impact of Inequality on Health in Canada: A Multi-Dimensional Framework," *Diversity & Equality in Health and Care* 7, no. 4 (2010),

In the pandemic era, mental health has been a crucial issue with people compelled to stay home and maintain social distancing. Loss of jobs has also exacerbated the problem. In this context, diaspora visible minorities are significantly affected compared to the White population. Moyser's analysis of a crowdsourced survey conducted by Statistics Canada from April 24 to May 11, 2020, on the mental health condition of the Canadian population proved this point. While Moyser explicitly stated that since the survey is crowdsourced and could not be a reliable basis for making inference of the whole population, it is still a good reference on the impact of COVID-19 situation of the mental health condition of visible minorities. The Statistic Canada survey made use of measurements on self-rated mental health, changes in mental health condition, and generalized anxiety disorder.[291] The study revealed that:

> Across most measures of mental health during the COVID-19 pandemic, participants from visible-minority groups had poorer outcomes than White participants. Although similar proportions of visible-minority and White participants reported that their mental health was "somewhat" or "much" worse since physical distancing began (51.3% and 52.2%, respectively), a greater proportion of participants from visible-minority groups reported "fair" or "poor" self-rated mental health (27.8% vs. 22.9%). Participants from visible-minority groups were also more likely to report symptoms consistent with "moderate" or "severe" generalized anxiety disorder in the two weeks prior to completing the survey (30.0% vs. 24.2%).[292]

Among the five largest visible minority groups (South Asian, Chinese, Black, Filipino, and Arab), South Asians have poorer health outcomes compared to the other groups on the three mental health measurements (except for Filipinos on generalized anxiety disorders).[293]

The relationship between health outcomes and race or ethnicity is of primordial concern in the light of the universal health care system of Canada that provides health access to all. Clearly, the previous studies alluded to reveal discrimination as determinant of health. In Halwani's research paper published by the Ontario Human Rights Commission, she stated that racial discrimination

---

https://diversityhealthcare.imedpub.com/abstract/the-impact-of-inequality-on-health-in-canada-a-multidimensional-framework-1943.html.

[291] Melissa Moyser, "The Mental Health of Population Groups Designated as Visible Minorities in Canada During the COVID-19 Pandemic," *Statistics Canada*, September 2, 2020, https://www150.statcan.gc.ca/n1/pub/45-28-0001/2020001/article/00077-eng.htm.

[292] Moyser, "The Mental Health of Population Groups."

[293] Moyser, "The Mental Health of Population Groups."

is not a direct determinant of health but socio-economic factors.[294] Race and ethnicity could not be discounted as factors in health outcomes as it was already delineated that diaspora visible minorities are struggling and even experiencing discrimination socially and economically. While stating this, Halwani added nuances to the issue of race or ethnicity in health by stating the problem of underrepresentation of racialized communities in the health care profession, problems in communication due to lack of minority languages in social and health services, and the lack of culturally sensitive care.[295] She opined that "equality of access is not ensured by uniformity in a multiracial society. Thus, culturally sensitive delivery of health care is a necessity if equality is to be a serious goal."[296]

Political and Social Participation

In the political and social spheres, the marginality of immigrants can be seen in their limited representation in the political system. A study by Han revealed that visible minorities are underrepresented in the House of Commons, which is the legislative branch of the Canadian political system. The study further looked into specific level of visible minority representation in the House of Commons which showed that "the percentage of visible minorities in the House is barely two-thirds of the visible minority population share in Canada. Indeed, visible minorities are numerically underrepresented in elected office."[297] He argued that such disproportional representation can be attributed to institutional and social factors. Institutional factors mainly reside on the issue of representation, particularly on the electoral system which limits such visible minority representation. As to social factors, one key barrier could be racial discrimination.[298] These include how race is framed in the media and racial hierarchy that both could frame visible minorities as of lesser status compared to White candidates.[299] He had cautioned however, that there needs to be a unified method to study "whether racial discrimination really contributes to visible minorities' underrepresentation in Canadian Parliament."[300]

Racial hierarchy is still a significant social issue faced by visible minorities that not only impact their political participation but also in other areas of

---

[294] Sana Halwani, "Racial Inequality in Access to Health Care Services," *Ontario Human Rights Commission*, December 2004, https://www.ohrc.on.ca/en/race-policy-dialogue-papers/racial-inequality-access-health-care-services.
[295] Halwani, "Racial Inequality."
[296] Halwani, "Racial Inequality."
[297] Jessie Han, "Institutional and Social Perspectives on Visible Minority Representation in Canadian Parliament," *Politicus Journal* (nd): 15.
[298] Han, "Institutional and Social Perspectives," 19-22.
[299] Han, "Institutional and Social Perspectives," 19-22.
[300] Han, "Institutional and Social Perspectives," 22.

integration in Canadian. The "possibility that visible minority candidates bearing non-native names may get discriminated against"[301] has also been mentioned earlier regarding the impact of their non-native names on their job applications. Overall, visible minorities still grapple with social exclusion despite the avowed multiculturalism policy that seeks to present Canadian society as a space where immigrants can flourish in their cultural or ethnic identities. While an overwhelming majority of immigrants had a strong sense of belonging to Canada,[302] there are strong indicators that visible minorities still lag in social inclusion and racial discrimination is still a factor to be addressed. The gradual shift of utilizing the concept of racialized groups to reflect the experience of visible minorities is a recognition of the reality of racial discrimination. In revealing this reality, Statistics Canada released data in support of Canada's Anti-Racism Strategy, that expressed the level of social inclusion of racialized groups using visible minority variables. The findings revealed that "while the rates of civic participation of racialized Canadians are generally similar to the rest of the population, their representation in management positions is considerably lower, and their voter turnout and political engagement are somewhat lower compared with other Canadians."[303] Definitely, there are variations in this civic participation between ethnic groups but it is sufficient to conclude that overall, visible minorities face barriers as they seek to integrate in Canadian society.

Summary

This chapter presents the history of marginality of diaspora visible minorities, their demographic characteristics, and specific experiences of discrimination and social exclusion. The data revealed that the experience of marginality of diaspora visible minorities is not a new phenomenon and that even in the present era, there are still significant integration barriers delineating racial discrimination, social exclusion, labour and health accessibility, and civic participation.

The presentation in this chapter is not only to delineate the nature and extent of marginality but to reveal the reality of such marginality based on data as objective evidence. While it is explained as a negative phenomenon, an integrative perspective presents a broader understanding beyond social

---

[301] Han, "Institutional and Social Perspectives," 19.

[302] Feng Hou, Grant Schellenberg, and John Berry, "Patterns and Determinants of Immigrants' Sense of Belonging to Canada and Their Source Country," October 18, 2016, https://www150.statcan.gc.ca/n1/pub/11f0019m/11f0019m2016383-eng.htm.

[303] Statistics Canada, "Portrait of the Social, Political and Economic Participation of Racialized Groups," May 17, 2022, https://www150.statcan.gc.ca/n1/daily-quotidien/220517/dq220517c-eng.htm.

conflict. The next chapter presents the missiological understanding of marginality and how this is essential in the leadership development of Christian diaspora visible minorities.

CHAPTER 7

MISSIOLOGICAL UNDERSTANDING OF MARGINALITY: TOWARDS THE DEVELOPMENT OF RELATIONAL MARGINALITY FOR LEADERSHIP DEVELOPMENT

Introduction

The previous chapter presented the experience and condition of marginality of diaspora visible minorities in Canada. It is a condition of powerlessness, inequality, and discrimination. This reality could not be overemphasized enough due to the negative impact of their vision for integration in Canadian society. Yet, biblical and scriptural foundations present a clear picture of God's redemptive and missiological purpose of marginality. Central to this purpose is God's act of redemption in Christ:

> Who, being in very nature God, did not consider equality with God something to be used to his own advantage; rather, he made himself nothing by taking the very nature of a servant, being made in human likeness. And being found in appearance as a man, he humbled himself by becoming obedient to death—even death on a cross![304]

As God's missiological medium, marginality is transformed into what the researchers coin as Relational Marginality.

Transformational Models of Marginality

Before elucidating further about relational marginality, it is important to provide a survey of transformative models of marginality. This survey provides foundation on the recognition that from a biblical and theological perspective, marginality is not just an adverse experience and condition as delineated in the review of multidisciplinary and social science perspectives.

New Marginality

Jung Young Lee coined the concept of new marginality to affirm the theological purpose of marginality of diaspora communities. His conception of marginality starts from his study of the liminal experience of being an Asian immigrant in the U.S. Having a Korean background, however, did not limit his theologizing on the Korean experience but delineated similarities of experience of other Asian

---

[304] Phil. 2: 6-8.

immigrants. He is thus speaking of his conception of multicultural theology from an experience of marginality. Thus, Lee stated that:

> Immigration is the most vivid and profound symbol of marginality for us. Through immigration, we are completely detached from a country that had protected and nurtured us. Immigration also estranges us from the centrality that previously protected us. We become displaced and must readjust our lives."[305]

Being an immigrant, for Lee, removes the stability that a person experiences of being in his country where he is at the center. It is from this idea of removal from centrality that he starts his theologizing. In being in another culture and being at the margins, he reflected that "marginality is only defined in relation to centrality. Without the center there is no margin."[306] He further observed that "this inclination to be at the center seems to be an intrinsic human drive."[307] He then sees the importance of getting perspective from the margin in understanding Christian faith.

In reflecting on his own migration journey, he delineated that his ethnicity is the most important determinant of marginality. He affirms the previous discussion in chapter 7 on the difference between race and ethnicity, where race should not be the basis in understanding marginality due to its artificial social construction nature imposed by people at the center. For him, "race is inclusive of ethnicity, just as culture is. Both racial and cultural characteristics are included in the ethnicity of marginal people."[308] His definition of marginality starts first with his reflection of the work of Park where an individual lives in two societies or cultures, but neither is a member of both. A marginal person is in an in-between state. This is similar to the concept of liminality where migrants are considered to be in a state of transition between two cultures.

---

[305] Lee, *Marginality*, 110.
[306] Lee, *Marginality*, 30.
[307] Lee, *Marginality*, 30.
[308] Lee, *Marginality*," 34.

Figure 1. In-Between (classical self-negating definition of marginality) [309]

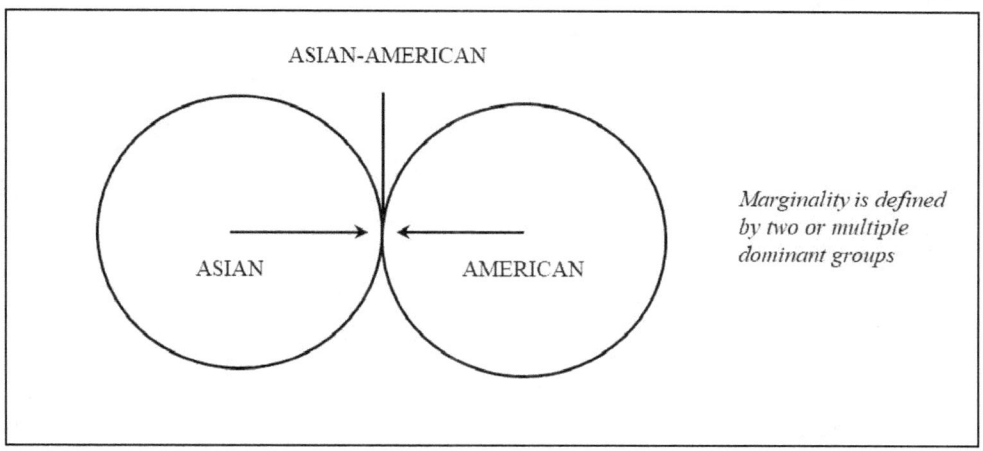

He contends, however, that while such definition of marginality is valid, it is conceived from the perspective of the dominant group rather from ethnic minorities.[310] He developed what he calls as a self-affirming definition of being an ethnic minority in a pluralistic society. He calls this idea as In-Both rather than In-Between.[311] To be In-Both is to accept the plurality of society where ethnocentrism is not the norm, nor can one be exclusivist. It seeks an appreciation of others.[312] Thus, "marginality imposes a new reality that transcends marginalization, for it means to be truly in both or in all worlds. The In-Both definition contends that a marginal person accepts both worlds without giving up either of the two cultures.

---

[309] Lee, *Marginality*, 57.
[310] Lee, *Marginality*, 47.
[311] Lee, *Marginality*, 49.
[312] Lee, *Marginality*, 50.

Figure 2. In-Both (self-affirming definition of marginality) [313]

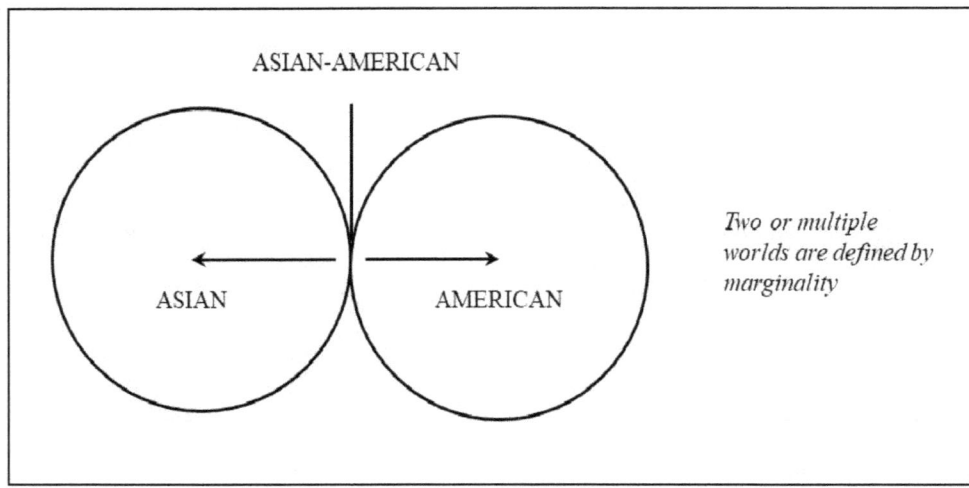

Lee goes further by delineating that both perspectives need to be integrated as a holistic definition of marginality or what he calls new marginality. In this perspective, he stated that both are two different aspects of reality.[314] He calls this In-Beyond where the margin and creative core belong to the same reality and are inseparable.[315] These are the negative and positive aspects of marginality.

The understanding of marginality as In-Beyond is important in Lee's postulation of the theology of marginality. He delineated that "if Jesus was the new marginal person who lived in-between and in-both, to have the mind of Jesus Christ means to think in terms of neither/nor and both/and. Likewise, to be a Christian means to be in the world but not of the world."[316]

---

[313] Lee, *Marginality"* 50.
[314] Lee, *Marginality*, 59.
[315] Lee, *Marginality*, 59.
[316] Lee, *Marginality*, 72.

Figure 3. In-Beyond (holistic definition of marginality) [317]

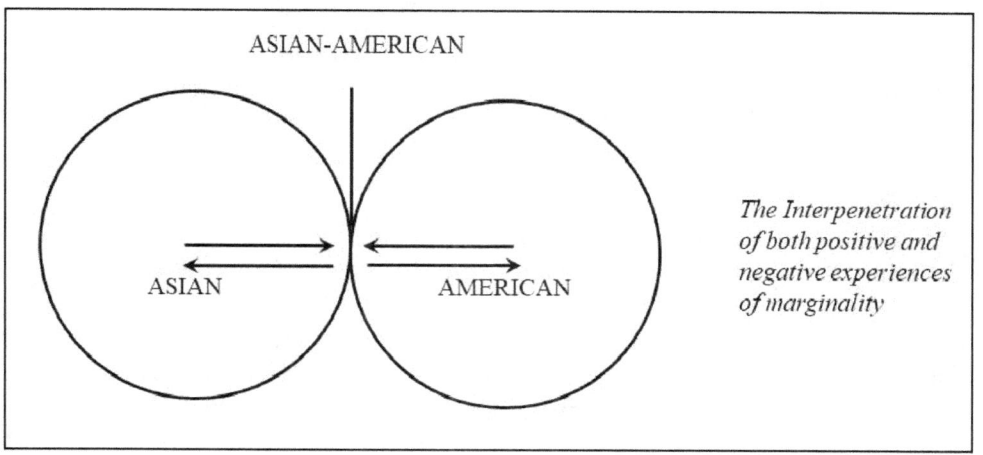

Christ is the epitome of the new marginality. Lee calls Christ as being in the margin of marginality. The core of this divine marginalization is the incarnation.[318] "Jesus was born as a marginal person."[319] It is interesting to note that God himself emphasized that his migration to humanity is not just an act of giving up his divinity but also of taking on the nature of a servant (Phil 2: 5-8). Lee notes that this is a significant act of marginality as a servant is an outsider "who is alienated from the world in which they live."[320] "Christ became as nothing."[321] The calling of Christian diaspora visible minorities, and for all Christians in this matter, is to follow Jesus' example of living in the margins as his life is a paradigm of new marginality.[322]

Positive Marginality

Woosung Calvin Choi coined the term "Positive Marginality" as a way of rethinking the classical concept of marginality to have an affirming homiletical paradigm in the current context of multiethnic congregations. Choi did not negate the contribution of the classical concept of marginality as a state of In-Between of individuals put forward by Park and Stonequist. As marginal persons are often portrayed as ethnic minorities, such classical definition is reflective of their experience. He conceives of positive marginality, however, to affirm the value of ethnic minorities by not considering themselves as victims

---

[317] Lee, *Marginality*, 60.
[318] Lee, *Marginality*, 79–83.
[319] Lee, *Marginality*, 78.
[320] Lee, *Marginality*, 82.
[321] Lee, *Marginality*, 82.
[322] Lee, *Marginality*, 83–90.

or outsiders or looking always from the lens of social conflict but as contributing members of society.[323] He, thus, provided a definition:

> Positive marginality is the ability to *Embrace* two or more ethnic and/or cultural groups, *Engage* in an intentional cross-cultural dialogue, *Establish* relationship with others by fully utilizing the assets and strengths of those groups, and thereby, *Embody* a communal identity and *Exhibit* a renewed vision for society.[324]

According to Choi, *Embrace* is more than proffering a spirit of accepting or welcoming but of seeing the importance of self and everyone in the image of God. "It refuses to view people through an ethnocentric lens; instead, it recognizes the common good and uniqueness of people. Racial and ethnic differences are viewed as the manifestation of divine creativity."[325] Furthermore, "*Embrace* involves acknowledging and respecting cultural integrity and its uniqueness and differences. Differences are not viewed as hindrances but as a vehicle to deepen the level of appreciation and respect."[326]

Engage involves going beyond self-boundaries and includes willingness to and intention for dialogue, having the spirit of reconciliation. Such spirit is not just about covering differences and conflicts but to be "concerned with the oppressed and empathizes with those who are socially marginalized to bring reconciliation, strength and transformation."[327] *Establish* is building "cross-cultural relationships" that are "mutually interdependent."[328] *Embody* seeks for communal identity by "educating and broadening one's multicultural perspective and finding one's identity in light of a larger sociocultural context of which one is a part."[329] *Exhibit* speaks of the commitment to go beyond self and serve others in love as revealed in Galatians 5: 13.[330]

Choi stated that his idea of Positive Marginality is anchored on the Double-Swing intercultural communication model of Yoshikawa where the latter's concept highlights the value of differences and otherness.[331] Such intercultural communication results to "existential leap" between partners and others. In

---

[323] Woosung Calvin Choi, *Preaching to Multiethnic Congregation: Positive Marginality as a Homiletical Paradigm* (New York: Peter Lang Inc., International Academic Publishers, 2015), 31.
[324] Choi, *Preaching to Multiethnic Congregation*, 32.
[325] Choi, *Preaching to Multiethnic Congregation*, 32.
[326] Choi, *Preaching to Multiethnic Congregation*, 32.
[327] Choi, *Preaching to Multiethnic Congregation*, 33.
[328] Choi, *Preaching to Multiethnic Congregation*, 33.
[329] Choi, *Preaching to Multiethnic Congregation*, 33.
[330] Choi, *Preaching to Multiethnic Congregation*, 33.
[331] Choi, *Preaching to Multiethnic Congregation*, 33-34.

this way, positive marginality creates "intentional dialogue" for "establishing relationships."

Choi lays out the five aspects of positive marginality on three key biblical foundations. The first is the Great Commission (Matt. 28: 18-20) where the command to go is essential in the calling to embrace and engage beyond one's social and cultural world. To make disciples is to establish genuine relationship and embody and exhibit common goal.[332]

He also based positive marginality in the Christian call to holiness. Choi understands that holiness is not just about separation but God's call for a "renewal vision of society." "This call to holiness does not exist in isolation but rather in the context of a community of faith that is in the reality of the "already and not yet."[333] Lastly, Choi underscored that the biblical concepts of aliens and strangers is reflective of positive marginality. He contends that the status of believers as aliens and strangers and therefore not citizens of this world calls up the idea of such holiness but at the same time engaging the world with a "positive attitude."[334]

Choi's conception of positive marginality is not just an embrace or engagement of others but engagement in a transformative way.

Relational Marginality

The delineation of transformative models of marginality are assertions that while marginality is a negative condition, Scripture redirects it to a life-affirming experience where God establishes his purpose for people on the move and at the same time is even reflective of his own salvific act in Christ. These two models are also foundational to the thesis of this study that diaspora marginality is central to God's purpose of reconciliation and redemption. It is the vehicle for his mission. This is the missiology of marginality.

The missiology of marginality stems from who God is—a relational Triune God who is in relationship with humanity, redeems humanity from sinfulness and transforms them in his image. In his sovereignty, God uses all human movements and even those distorted by sin, as a vehicle for his redemption. In the same manner that migration or the movement of people has been a providence in God's plan for plurality and scattering of the nations, marginality is essential to his mission.

Marginality could only be providentially understood in the context of relationships. From his relationship with his creation (vertical), he calls his redeemed people to live out such redemption in a spirit of loving relationship to others (horizontal), even to those who are persecutorial towards believers

---

[332] Choi, *Preaching to Multiethnic Congregation*, 76-77.
[333] Choi, *Preaching to Multiethnic Congregation*, 78.
[334] Choi, *Preaching to Multiethnic Congregation*, 79- 80.

(Matt. 5: 40-44; Lk. 6: 29). This is relational marginality. <u>Relational marginality is a state of being that affirms that the exclusionary nature of marginality is the vehicle of God's redemptive purpose that exhibits his kingdom value of servanthood and enables his people to be in submission with him who is the center and be in relationship with everyone in a transformative manner.</u>

Relational marginality is not acquiescence to exclusion, discrimination, and injustice that diaspora visible minorities experience from the majority culture. It has already been delineated that God seeks justice and believers must work for a just world as God is a God of justice that seeks to liberate his people from the clutches of unbridled use of power. This is also a recognition that in this world, people are subjects to powerful forces that oppress and discriminate. These forces are both of human origin and spiritual forces of evil (Eph. 6: 12) and are beyond the control of the marginalized to change.

Yet it is in this condition of powerlessness and marginality that God reveals his missional purpose. The state of marginality of immigrants needs to be understood in the context of God's mission. From this perspective, marginality is not just an issue of justice and a push to shift the dynamics of power relations to liberate immigrants from such a state but to understand the message of God and his desire for his creation through this experience. The missiological principle here is that immigrants are called into a new marginality of being Christ's followers. It is to be liberated to serve Christ. I affirm what Lee states that for the followers of Christ, "liberation from the margin does not mean to be at the center that dominates the margin. Liberation means to transfer one form of marginality to another form of marginality, that is, to transfer from the marginality of human centrality to the new marginality of divine presence in the world."[335]

Conceptual Framework

The previous chapters explored the biblical, scriptural, and theological foundations of marginality, and delineated the nature of ethnic identity of visible diaspora minorities. In both explorations of marginality and ethnicity of visible minorities, it is evident that these are anchored on the nature of God and his redemptive purpose. While the social sciences conceive of these as products of social realities with consequent negative impacts in the lives of diaspora visible minorities, their ethnic identities, migration journeys, and experience of exclusion are central to God's divine plan and even reflective of his nature. In order to understand the missiological purpose of the ethnicities and marginality of visible minorities, it is important to review relational paradigm as the foundation of relational marginality.

---

[335] Lee, *Marginality*, 101–2.

Relational Realism and Relational Marginality

Relational realism is defined as "The systematic understanding that 'reality' is primarily based on the 'vertical relationship' between God and the created world and secondarily 'horizontal relationship' with the created order."[336] Reality is based on the trinitarian nature of God as the basis of all relationships as expressed by the relational pattern between the Father, Son, and Holy Spirit (Immanent Trinity). From this trinitarian relationship proceeds God's relationship with his creation (Economic Trinity) or what the paradigm calls as the vertical relationship. This relationship is the basis for mission that delineates the horizontal relationship among created beings.

To understand the uniqueness of the relational paradigm, it is best to have a brief survey of epistemological shifts in the conception of reality. By epistemology, we mean the "cognitive assumptions underlying certain perspectives" or worldview.[337] The first cognitive view has been the result of scientific method that utilizes empirical evidence in coming up with reality. Reality in this case is objective and independent of human perception. As a reaction to the limitations of positivism, functionalism became the dominant perspective of reality where it relies more on subjective preference rather than objective reality. A third shift occurred that tried to balance the previous two perspectives—critical realism. Critical realism offers a middle ground between positivism which emphasizes objective truth, and instrumentalism, which stresses subjective nature of human knowledge.[338] It assumes that there is a real world independent of human perception (realism) but it examines this reality by the process of the mind's acquisition of this knowledge (critical). In this sense, all knowledge has objective and subjective dimensions.

In making a clean break from these epistemologies, Wan argues that reality is a result of God's creation and that there are only two categories of existence: the creator and the created order.

---

[336] Wan and Hedinger, *Relational Missionary Training*, 17.
[337] Paul Hiebert, *Missiological Implications of Epistemological Shifts: Affirming Truth in a Modern/Postmodern World.* (Harrisburg, PA: Trinity Press International, 1999), 1.
[338] Hiebert, *Missiological Implications of Epistemological Shifts*, 69.

Figure 4. Creator and Creature in Relation to Each Other[339]

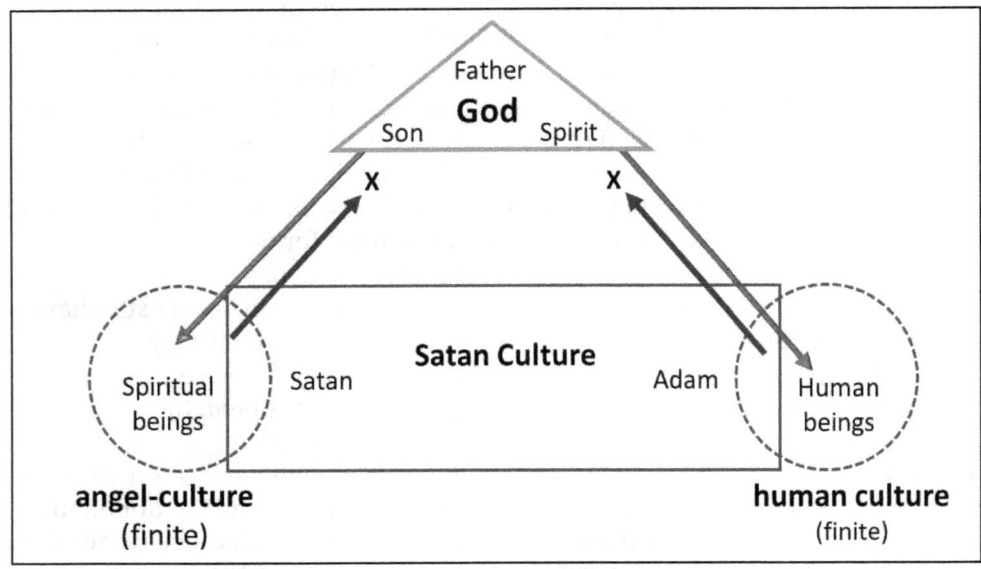

In defining the immanent Trinity, it specifies the relationship of God within the Trinity or how the members of the Trinity relate to one another.[340] In this reality alone, it specifies that the nature of God is relational. In this relationship of the three persons in the Trinity, the Latin Fathers used the term *perichoresis* where "all members are involved in personal and dynamic ways."[341]

Of specific importance is how relational realism provides a clear delineation of reality as expressing the excluded middle. Scripture is clear that "our struggle is not against flesh and blood, but against the rulers, against the authorities, against the powers of this dark world."[342] As mentioned earlier, Hiebert made a crucial conception of the excluded middle or the reality of the spiritual realms in understanding reality and how this impacts not only people's worldview but its power and consequences in human relations.[343]

Relational Interactionism and Relational Marginality

A significant result of Wan's Relational Realism is the development of Relational Interactionism as a framework in defining the patterns of relationships between the Triune God and created beings. In particular,

---

[339] Wan and Hedinger, *Relational Missionary Training*, 19.
[340] Wan and Hedinger, *Relational Missionary Training*, 21.
[341] Wan and Hedinger, *Relational Missionary Training*, 22.
[342] Eph. 6: 12.
[343] Hiebert, "The Flaw of the Excluded Middle," 35-37.

"Relational Interactionism is an interdisciplinary framework developed from practical considerations of interaction of personal Beings/beings forming realistic relational network, in multiple contexts, and with various consequences."[344] The framework proffers that any human or social relationships could only be understood and find meaning within the relationship of the three persons in the Trinity. In this relationship of the three persons in the Trinity, the Latin Fathers used the term *perichoresis* where "all members are involved in personal and dynamic ways."[345] *Perichoresis* speaks of the mutual indwelling of the three persons of the Trinity where: "first, the three persons of the Trinity are all fully in one another. And second, each person of the Trinity is in full possession of the divine essence."[346] Furthermore, "the inter-communion of the persons is reciprocal, and their operations are inseparable."[347]

From this relationship within the Trinity, the Triune God proceeds to form relationship with people who are in reconciliation with him, or as Jesus prayed, "that all of them may be one, Father, just as you are in me and I am in you. May they also be in us so that the world may believe that you have sent me" (John. 17: 21). The importance of Relational Interactionism in defining an integrative concept of marginality is its iteration that it is the result of breakdown of relationship between the Triune God and his created beings, which then results of destruction of relationships on a horizontal level. The issues of power dynamics, socio-economic disparity, injustice, racism, and cultural marginalization are products of a deeper problem of human rebellion and sin, and are descriptive of individual, institutional, and societal actions that miss relational markers derived from a relational and just God. Marginality is a relational issue.

Relational Transformation and Relational Marginality

A key contribution of Relational Interactionism is its conception of transformational change and transgressional change as diverging results of relational dynamics with the Triune God. Transformational change is the "dynamism and process of positive change, originating vertically from the Triune God and ushered in the relational reality horizontally, through the process of interaction between personal Beings (the Triune God) and human beings, at micro and macro (personal and institutional) levels and multiple

---

[344] Wan and Raibley, *Transformational Change in Christian Ministry*, 9.
[345] Wan and Hedinger, *Relational Missionary Training*, 22.
[346] Kevin Deyoung, "Theological Primer: Perichoresis," *The Gospel Coalition*, November 19, 2020, https://www.thegospelcoalition.org/blogs/kevin-deyoung/theological-primer-perichoresis/.
[347] Deyoung, "Theological Primer."

dimensions (i.e., spiritual, moral, social, and behavioral),"[348] while transgressional change is the change caused by the enemy of the Triune God and are thereby "contrary to the attributes of God and his will."[349] Marginality, in all its negative, unjust, and discriminatory characteristics are manifestations of transgressional change. It is a product and consequence of human transgression against the Triune God and the resulting fallen nature and sinfulness. It is the consequences of a broken (vertical) relationship which results in fragmentation and brokenness (horizontal) in human relations.

As stated earlier, marginality is a reflection and result of transgressional change. In delineating marginality as transgressional change, it is then appropriate to understand human relational dynamics as just symptomatic rather than causal in nature. Thus, for a people who are in relationship with the Triune God, marginality is not just a problem to be solved but a providential reality to be lived under his redemptive purpose. Any human action to resolve transgressional change does not take into consideration the deeper problem of human depravity. Thus, in God's redemptive act, marginality is transformed as his agency for redemption. The cross is the greatest manifestation of his intentional act to experience marginality and transform it into his salvific act. In the same manner, marginality could be transformed by God for his redemptive purpose.

Christian immigrants then have a significant place in directing people to be Christ-followers and be subject to his lordship. Their experience serves as a vehicle of God's message that he has the sole claim to centrality. Following Christ enables immigrants to teach that all God's people are foreigners on this earth (1 Pet. 1: 17-21) and their experience of marginality follows Christ's migration journey from heaven and takes the form of a servant (Phil. 2: 5-8). Christian immigrant leadership is then a must to lead church formation into its exilic identity and direct missional efforts towards the new marginality based on their lived experience. For Christ-follower immigrants to be the "divine presence in the world," their leadership development becomes a necessity, not to create a place of centrality, but of directing people into this relational marginality in Christ.

Missiological Implications of Relational Marginality

Relational Marginality as Agency for Mission

It is important to reiterate what Lee stated that Christ is the epitome of the new marginality and that the core of this divine marginalization is the incarnation.[350]

---

[348] Wan, "Relational Transformational Leadership."
[349] Wan and Raibley, *Transformational Change in Christian Ministry*, 7.
[350] Lee, *Marginality*, 79–83.

As God became marginal in Christ, the calling of all God's people is to follow this example of living in the margins. Paul categorically calls believers to imitate Christ's humility:

> In your relationships with one another, have the same mindset as Christ Jesus: Who, being in very nature God, did not consider equality with God something to be used to his own advantage; rather, he made himself nothing by taking the very nature of a servant, being made in human likeness. And being found in appearance as a man, he humbled himself by becoming obedient to death—even death on a cross![351]

Imitating Christ's humility is not acquiescence to injustice of exclusion and discrimination but of exhibiting Christlikeness in all situations. To live in the margins is to live Christ's life even amid the experience and condition of societal marginality. A parallel understanding of experience of marginality is on the issue of submission to slavery in 1 Peter 2: 18-20.

John Piper appropriately understood this as not acquiescence to slavery but consideration of the ultimacy of Christ's lordship no matter what condition one finds himself in subjection to human institutions, whether one is a wife or husband, a citizen, or a slave.[352] In claiming that Christ is the ultimate master, it relativizes authority of human masters as Christ is the ultimate master.[353] For Piper, "this is a radically Christian kind of submission."[354] Of primary importance is the act of doing good.[355] While diaspora marginality could never be equated with slavery, the scriptural message is that no human institutions or conditions could claim ultimate subjection to a believer. Freedom in Christ supersedes all human negative conditions that enslaves and dehumanizes.

In these conditions, believers are to do good and exhibit Christlike behavior as expression of his lordship and ultimate claim. In this expression of doing good and being Christlike, one manifests how one is subject to the Lordship of Christ, the only master who can claim centrality. Relational marginality recognizes that a believer is in relationship with a Triune God who himself intentionally stepped into marginality to claim lordship and redeem his creation. God's act of marginality in Christ is an act of mission. In the same manner, the diaspora believer's recognition of his marginality as reflection of Christ's marginality relativizes the power of unjust social structures and elevates the power and centrality of Christ. Believers are to exhibit humility and continue to do good as an example that invites people to accept the lordship

---

[351] Phil. 2: 5-8.
[352] John Piper, "Slaves, Obey Your Masters; 1 Peter 2:18–20, Part 1," *Desiring God*, January 14, 2016, https://www.desiringgod.org/labs/slaves-obey-your-masters.
[353] Piper, "Slaves, Obey Your Masters."
[354] Piper, "Slaves, Obey Your Masters."
[355] 1 Pet. 3: 9; 1 Pet. 4: 19.

and centrality of Christ. In exhibiting Christlike character and doing good, a believer models the newness of life in Christ in contrast to the prevailing patterns of the world. Relational marginality is an agency for mission.

Relational Marginality as a Template for Christian Living

It was expressed earlier in Chapter 5 that both migration and marginality are expressions of Christian calling to make God as the center. Jesus delineated this centrality of God in a relational manner through his summary of the Commandments (Matt. 22: 36-40). Loving one's neighbor is predicated on one's love for God. As God is the center, Christian life is a call to dependence and faith and be in relationship with the Triune God. Relational marginality is a transformed marginality that is not the product of social exclusion and discrimination but on the reality of Christ's being as the center of all things. As a result of his humbling act of taking the form of a slave and dying on the cross (Phil. 2: 6-8), God affirmed his centrality where "God exalted him to the highest place and gave him the name that is above every name, that at the name of Jesus every knee should bow, in heaven and on earth and under the earth, and every tongue acknowledge that Jesus Christ is Lord, to the glory of God the Father."[356]

All Christians are called into a life of being foreigners in this world, living a life dependent on God. As Peter says, we are to live as foreigners in this world and express this as badge of being Christ-followers (1 Pet. 2: 11-25). As diaspora visible minorities can endure migration and marginality, all believers can carry this exilic and marginal existence template of Christian living. As God journeyed from heaven and lived a marginal existence on earth, then believers are to follow this path of relational marginality. The condition of marginality of diaspora visible minorities is a significant experience that they endure and a message they bring to all Christ-followers that the experiences of migration and marginality are articulation of God's salvific act. Believers are called to live a distinct and honorable living regardless of their conditions on this earth. Marginality is not a condition to be endured but a life to be lived with distinction. Marginality is a Kingdom value.

Christian Diaspora Visible Minorities as Agents of God's Mission

There is sufficient data of migrants becoming missionaries in countries where they work. God made migration to be a vehicle for his mission to the nations with believers serving as agents of the gospel. In their experience of marginality, diaspora visible minorities should utilize their lived experience of marginality as a reflection of the Triune God's own migration from heaven and take the form of a slave. Their lived experience puts them in a truly unique

---

[356] Phil. 2: 9-11.

position to be messengers of a God who intentionally stepped into a marginal state to bring his people back in relationship with him.

This does not negate the calling of all believers as agents of mission. The diaspora visible minorities' experience of migration and marginality constitutes a significant missional calling as theirs is a lived experience. It is thereby expedient for migrants and Christian diaspora visible minorities to be equipped in mission to the host countries, the diaspora communities, and the people on the move. Such equipping of diaspora visible minorities must be anchored on their identities. It has been mentioned in chapter 7 that ethnicity is a significant issue for the marginality of visible minorities. In their distinction of being considered as the 'other,' it is appropriate to focus their missional calling as anchored not just on their migration and marginal experience but on their ethnic identities.

In the current milieu, ethno-cultural identity is one of the major drivers of politics, together with national, religious, racial, gender, and sexual identities.[357] As a reaction to globalization, people had utilized such identities in promoting a sense of otherness where those who are not part of such a group are considered "the other." Wolf observed that such reaction has been exclusionary in nature.[358] In that act of exclusion, violence, injustice, oppression, and discrimination are expressions of treating others who do not share the identities or characteristics of the reference group. As a contrast to this exclusionary tendency, Wolf proposes to define these identity differences as a medium for embrace. He thus posits the premise that "God's reception of hostile humanity into divine communion is a model for how human beings should relate to the other."[359] While Wolf has a broader theological conception of embrace beyond the issue of the concern of this book on the role of Christian diaspora people in mission, his theological reflection of embrace as anchored on the "perichoresis" of the Trinity is a useful tool in the social application of identity and self-donation.[360] In this regard, equipping Christian diaspora visible minorities in mission needs to be anchored on their ethnic identities as the fulcrum for embracing other diaspora peoples. In the Canadian multicultural context, the act of 'embracing' the 'other' carries significant weight in bridging the ethno-cultural divide.

---

[357] Miroslav Wolf, *Exclusion and Embrace: A Theological Exploration of Identity, Otherness, and Reconciliation* (Nashville, TN: Abingdon Press, 2019), xiv.
[358] Wolf, *Exclusion and Embrace*, 49-96."
[359] Wolf, *Exclusion and Embrace*, 98.
[360] Wolf, *Exclusion and Embrace*, 343-367.

Leadership Development of Diaspora Visible Minorities: From Marginality to Relational Marginality

The state of marginality of diaspora individuals and communities calls for transformative change. This necessitates understanding of their current state of marginality to create a new meaning of such marginality. As mentioned in chapter 2, for Christian diaspora individuals and communities, their relationship with God and his household (*oikos*) creates a new meaning of their foreigner status (*paroikos*) and state of marginality as a condition of value and dignity.

Christian immigrants then have a significant place in directing people to be Christ-followers and be subject to his lordship. Their experience serves as a vehicle of God's message that he has the sole claim to centrality. Following Christ enables immigrants to teach that all God's people are foreigners on this earth (1 Pet. 1: 17-21) and their experience of marginality follows Christ's migration journey from heaven and takes the form of a servant (Phil. 2: 5-8). Christian immigrant leadership is then a must to lead church formation into its exilic identity and direct missional efforts towards the new marginality based on their lived experience`. For Christ-follower immigrants to be the "divine presence in the world," their leadership development becomes a necessity, not to create a place of centrality, but of directing people into this new mode of marginality. For Christian immigrants to be the missionaries of the new marginality, a relational transformational leadership development presents a viable path of discipleship. Leadership development is the process of equipping Christian diaspora leaders to perform their roles as agents of relational marginality. As agents of a relational Triune God who seeks to redeem a sinful humanity, Christian diaspora leaders are to express relational leadership to influence others to accept the reconciling act of a relational God and become Christ-followers.

Formation of a Hermeneutical Community

The theology of migration and marginality must be rooted in scripture. Such scriptural basis of theologizing, according to Hiebert, is grounded on the fact that scripture is God's revelation rather than human reflection about God.[361] From this perspective, a clear enunciation of God's salvific purpose for migration and marginality as revealed in scripture has to be done.

God built his salvation history through the migration of his people. In this migration journey, it was also directing them in the space of marginality. Lee states that:

---

[361] Hiebert, *Missiological Implications of Epistemological Shifts*, 101.

Immigration is the most vivid and profound symbol of marginality for us. Through immigration, we are completely detached from a country that had protected and nurtured us. Immigration also estranges us from the centrality that previously protected us. We become displaced and must readjust our lives."[362]

Thus, his act of redemption is integrating both migration and marginality as means to attain his purpose.

Yet biblical interpretation is also influenced by people's cultural backgrounds and lead to theological differentiation. Similarly, different diaspora ethnic communities would have different perspectives of their experience and biblical interpretations. Hiebert proposes that due to cultural biases, "theologizing must be done in community."[363] Kraus calls this a "community of interpretation" or "hermeneutical community."[364] He further notes:

> Principles of interpretation are important, but secondary. There needs to be an authentic correspondence between gospel announced and a "new order" embodied in community for scripture to play its proper roles as part of the original witness. The authentic community is the hermeneutical community. It determines the actual enculturated meaning of scriptures.[365]

Diaspora peoples have shared experience, and scriptural reflection should also be a shared one to reflect on the similarities of their journey. Hermeneutical endeavor is to reflect on the understanding of God's purpose for migration and the consequent marginality and then apply this in their current experience.

A hermeneutical community is a community that does not only interpret and reflect on scripture together but an effort to reflect on the purpose of a God who seeks to be in relationship with his people. In this interpretation, diaspora Christians will realize that God is calling them to reflect on their experience and transpose these into the proper scriptural meaning that points to God's purpose for their experience in the light of the biblical truth. The experience of marginality needs to be understood by diaspora peoples that this is an experience of the Triune God who intentionally migrated from heaven to earth and became a servant (Phil. 2: 5-8). Thus, such interpretation and theologizing by a hermeneutical community needs to be grounded on the relational framework to avoid what Hiebert warns as theological relativism and

---

[362] Lee, *Marginality*, 110.
[363] Hiebert, *Missiological Implications of Epistemological Shifts*, 102.
[364] Norman C. Kraus, *The Authentic Witness: Credibility and Authority* (Grand Rapids: Eerdmans, 1979), 71.
[365] Kraus, *The Authentic Witness*, 71.

privatization of faith.[366] It is only in relationship with the Triune God that the community receive genuine revelation and inspiration.

Figure 5. Relational Marginality in the Context of Hermeneutical Community

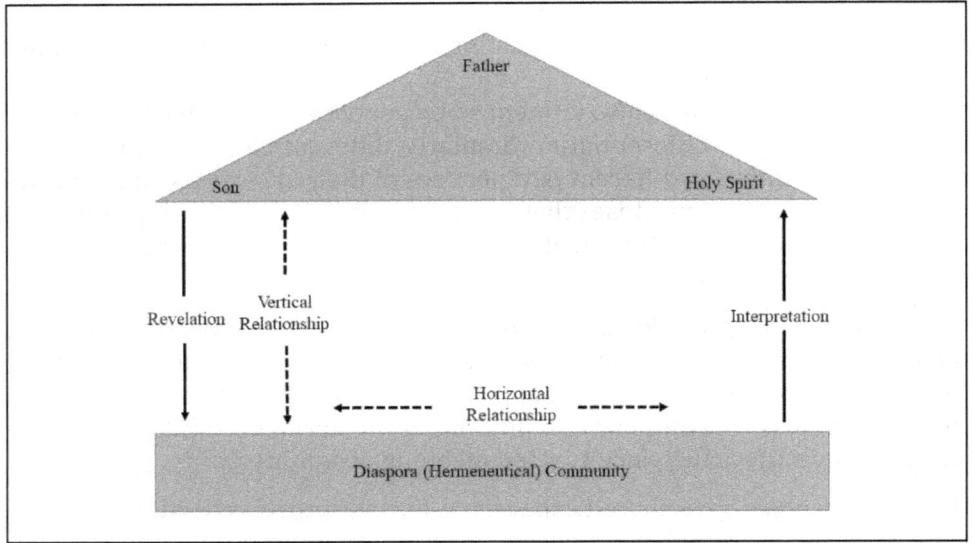

As shown in figure 6, it is the Triune God who reveals himself in scripture. It is thus paramount to understand that such revelation is an act of God to be in relationship with peoples. The use of scripture for training and equipping is dependent on the reality that all scripture is inspired by God (2 Tim. 3: 16-17). It is only in relationship with him that he will reveal his truth (Mk. 4: 10-20). In the same vein, it is in human relationships that God further concretizes this truth. Thus, any interpretation of scripture is to be grounded in this vertical and horizontal axis of relationships. As a result of the vertical relationship, such interpretation necessitates a call for *koinonia* and *ekklesia*.

It's important to note how Paul encouraged the Philippians in chapter 2, that their relationship with one another should be patterned after God's intentional act of migration and marginality. In understanding scripture together, and God's purpose for migration and marginality, diaspora peoples are also called to reflect on their experience, not of marginalization but of being called to be leaders and teachers in decentering humanity as emphasized by Paul's hymn to the Philippians that Christ is the only one worthy to be at the center (Phil. 2: 9-11).

It is then imperative that leadership development requires competency beyond biblical interpretation which is the common initiative in the western

---

[366] Hiebert, *Missiological Implications of Epistemological Shifts*, 102.

context. It seems that academic training in biblical interpretation, and even perhaps proficiency on systematic theology, is the norm for competency and expertise. In reflecting on what Kraus stipulated earlier, "principles of interpretation are important, but secondary."[367] The correspondence between the "gospel announced, and a 'new order' embodied in community" requires leaders that are well versed in cultural reflection and capacity to gather collective ideas on their community condition. The development of a hermeneutical community requires leaders who are relational and who make relationship as the foundation for biblical interpretation and reflection.

Development of Intercultural Competency

An operationalization of a hermeneutical community in the context of relational paradigm calls for different ethnic communities to cross cultural boundaries and create avenues for Bible reflection in such cross-cultural and intercultural contexts. The importance of this step in relational leadership could not be overestimated in the light of the fact that most diaspora churches and communities in Canada are monocultural church formations with limited ways of crossing cultural boundaries. The tendency of diaspora churches to be monocultural is natural in view of people's inclination to be with their own kind. Yet, a disturbing trend in Canada is that this monocultural tendency could be caused by marginalization. Aside from the experience of racial discrimination, host churches are also wanting in their efforts to welcome and integrate diaspora Christians.

In reflecting on Lau's research on the impact of Canada's multiculturalism policy on intercultural church formation, he surmised that this would have influence on ethnic diversity in Evangelical churches, and concomitantly intercultural competency. Lau's study revealed that such policy is not the main driver of inclusivity but the gospel call. The "acceptance of 'aliens and strangers' by Canadian Christians was revealed to be motivated by adherence to Scriptural tenets of 'loving one's neighbour' and the view that all humans are bearers of God's image rather than promoting a politics of recognition and equality."[368] In this regard, the move towards intercultural competency is not influenced by external factors but by scriptural foundations and values that compel churches to cross mono-cultural tendencies. This gives further credence to the necessity for the formation of hermeneutical communities.

The need for the formation of a hermeneutical community among diaspora peoples presents challenges in the light of multiple cultural domains where experience and interpretation of marginality varies between cultures. Yet it is in this diversity that the formation of a hermeneutical community becomes a

---

[367] Kraus, *The Authentic Witness*, 71.
[368] Lau, "The Influence of Canadian Multiculturalism on Ethnic Diversity," 116.

necessity to enable the sharing of experiences and search for biblical truth together, leading to a universal acceptance of truth beyond cultural nuances. The formation of a community of interpretation involves identification of leaders among the diverse diaspora communities who will serve in bringing universal scriptural principles back to their respective communities. The Relational framework already provides a key tool in developing diaspora leaders to be agents for the formation of a hermeneutical community. Thus, relationship is the key! Bringing ethnically diverse communities together to reflect on scripture in light of their experience requires what Hiebert calls cultural mediators or, "those who stand between different communities and cultures."[369] In view of his perspective on cultural mediators as grounded on contextualization, this could well be a basis for the formation of a hermeneutical community. Thus, he further states:

> To minister effectively as a mediator among different cultures, a person must become a transcultural person with a well-integrated metacultural identity. People who identify only with their own community will not be trusted by another.[370]

Identifying diaspora Christian leaders to be cultural mediators requires intercultural competency and the development of bicultural identity. Intercultural competence involves "increasing cultural self-awareness; deepening understanding of the experiences, values, perceptions, and behaviors of people from diverse cultural communities; and expanding the capability to shift cultural perspective and adapt behavior to bridge across cultural differences."[371] Being an immigrant does not automatically make one interculturally competent. Those who pursue integration or bicultural identity have such skills in adjusting to different cultures owing to their posture of acceptance of these cultures. Bicultural identity is the person's ability "to embrace values from the host and home cultures and engage in positive intercultural exchange."[372]

The development of intercultural competency and bicultural identity is anchored on transformational change brought about through the relationship

---

[369] Paul G. Hiebert, *The Gospel in Human Contexts: Anthropological Explorations for Contemporary Missions* (Grand Rapids, Michigan: Baker Academics, 2009), 179.

[370] Hiebert, *The Gospel in Human Contexts*, 185.

[371] Mitchell R. Hammer, "The Intercultural Development Inventory: A New Frontier in Assessment and Development of Intercultural Competence," in *Student Learning Abroad*, ed. M. Vande Berg, R.M. Paige, and K.H. Lou (Sterling, VA: Stylus Publishing, 2012), 115–136.

[372] Tony Wu, "Bicultural Identity," in *Encyclopedia of Child Behavior and Development*, ed. Sam Goldstein and Jack A. Naglieri (Boston, MA: Springer US, 2011), 238–239, https://doi.org/10.1007/978-0-387-79061-9_331.

with the Triune God. This transformation goes beyond Mezirow's transformative learning which is based on reflecting on prior experience to determine future course of action. Beyond Mezirow, we see a process of a growing relationship with the Triune God as the basis of experiential reflection. The relationship with God creates new ways of understanding reality even beyond negative experiences of marginality. Developing intercultural competency is anchored on how God enables rather than a self-enabling process.

The first act of the Holy Spirit after the ascension of Jesus was to touch the lives of the disciples by enabling them to speak in different languages and enabling God-fearing Jews to hear the gospel in their specific languages (Acts 2: 1-40). The Holy Spirit's work was an act of developing intercultural competency among these early church leaders. They became the "nucleus of churches in most of the cities where Paul went."[373]

Thus, leadership development within the diaspora hermeneutical community is a product primarily of the Triune God's enabling towards intercultural competence and secondarily, on the individual leader's intercultural experience and reflection within such community. As shown in figure 7, the Triune God enables the transformation of a leader to develop intercultural competency. The reflection and experience of a leader in a hermeneutical community also shapes and impacts this transformation.

---

[373] Pierson, *The Dynamics of Christian Mission*, 43-44.

Figure 6. Leadership Development in a Relational Framework

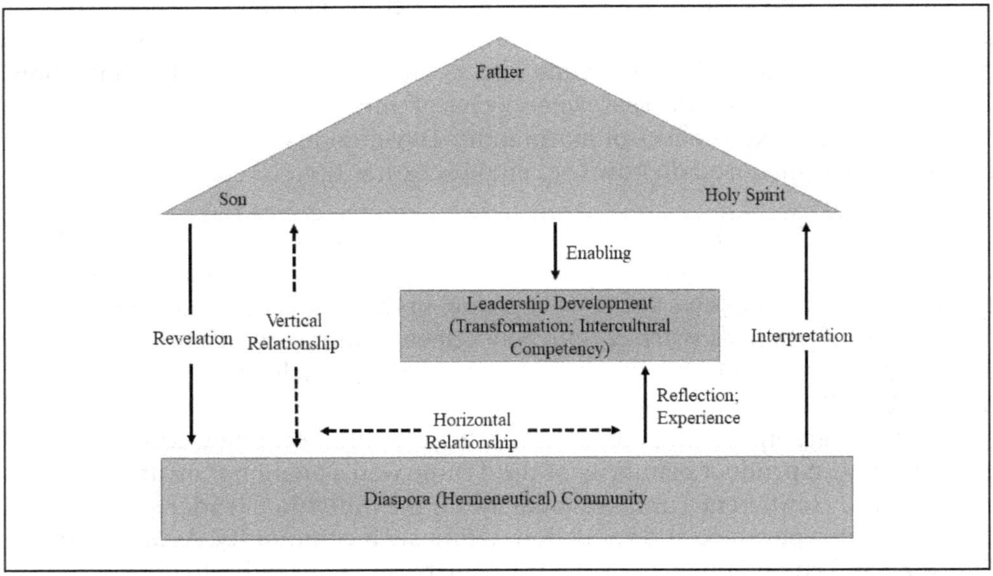

Diagram: A house-shaped framework with "Father" at the apex (roof), "Son" on the left and "Holy Spirit" on the right. Below are labeled arrows showing "Revelation" and "Vertical Relationship" on the left, "Enabling" flowing down to a central box labeled "Leadership Development (Transformation; Intercultural Competency)", and "Interpretation" on the right. A "Reflection; Experience" arrow flows upward. A "Horizontal Relationship" arrow runs horizontally at the bottom, above a box labeled "Diaspora (Hermeneutical) Community".

Formation of Intercultural Teams

This portion is based on the ideas of Stallard and Hill. Stallard puts forward the thesis that effective mission and ministry in an urban multicultural setting requires the formation of diverse leadership teams as patterned in the book of Acts.[374] It could be understood then that intercultural transformation happens when there is intentionality in forming multiculturally or ethnically diverse teams. Thus, he stated that "the presence of such patterns in Luke's narrative probably suggests to the reader that it would be wise to consider the multicultural team model when ministering in settings that are contextually similar to the settings in the book of Acts. This means that multicultural ministry teams are, as many have noted, a best practice for many multicultural environments."[375]

What is significant to this book, however, Stallard's reference to the work of Daniel Hill about the need to address power dynamics in intercultural teams.[376] Before delving into Hill's thoughts, we need to briefly revisit the idea of power dynamics that was discussed earlier in this book. As mentioned, Averil Bell argues that the integration of immigrants or diaspora communities into a host society carries with it "a complex and power-laden set of relations between

---

[374] Stallard, "The Development of Multicultural Teams in the Book of Acts."
[375] Stallard, "The Development of Multicultural Teams in the Book of Acts," 201.
[376] See in Stallard, "The Development of Multicultural Teams in the Book of Acts," 2.

people and places."[377] Oftentimes, these power dynamics are also present in church and mission leadership settings. Thus, "the most critical dynamic revolves around how power is shared."[378] He further claimed that "the locus of intercultural transformation revolves around the navigation of power. Each congregation needs to develop a plan for how it will explore historical power dynamics and implement a system for sharing power across diverse constituencies."[379]

How is this idea of power dynamics in intercultural or diverse team related to relational marginality? Primarily, intercultural or diverse teams are important in ensuring representation and inclusion of Christian diaspora visible minorities in church and mission leadership. Marginality in church and mission settings happens when visible minorities are not given leadership roles and are not given voice. Representation and inclusion are acts of relationality. This should not just be tokenism, however, but genuine desire in creating equitable and equal leadership spaces for diaspora visible minorities. There needs to be equality in relationships.

The principles of Hill in creating equitable and equal relationships for leadership development of Christian diaspora visible minorities are significant and worth specifying in this regard:[380]

- Principle 1: Embrace a team leadership model.
- Principle 2: Create an environment where leaders come fully as they are.
- Principle 3: Establish a consensus-based approach to decision-making.
- Principle 4: Mutually commit to authentic conflict resolution.
- Principle 5: Remain on the lookout for tokenism.
- Principle 6: Be mindful of the Acts 6 model.
- Principle 7: Emphasize the importance of solving problems together.
- Principle 8: Submit to a common vision.
- Principle 9: Develop a set of values that adheres the leadership team together.
- Principle 10: Cultivate an atmosphere of love.

In referring to the "Acts 6 model" in principle 6, Hill alluded to the issue at play in Acts 6 where the food-sharing program created by the apostles led to complaint by Hellenistic Jews that their widows were being overlooked in favor

---

[377] Bell, "Being 'at Home' in the Nation," 240.
[378] Daniel Hill, "Just Power: Ten Principles for Building Intercultural Leadership Teams," in *Intercultural Ministry: Hope for a Changing World*, ed. Grace Ji-Sun Kim and Jann Aldredge-Clanton (Valley Forge, PA: Judson Press, 2017), 111.
[379] Hill, "Just Power," 123.
[380] Hill, "Just Power," 113–123.

of the widows of Hebrew origin.[381] They created a solution where the marginalized group was empowered to solve their own problems that led to the emergence of leaders among them.[382]

The development of intercultural or diverse teams is an important process of leadership formation among diaspora visible minority leaders. It creates a space of acceptance and affirmation of their voices and gifts.

Leading from Marginality to Relational Marginality

The movement from marginality to relational marginality is a process of transformation where diaspora communities can understand their experience of being in the margins as central to the message of God in decentering humanity so that they would be under his lordship as God alone has claim to centrality.

Yet from this experience of marginality, God is assuring diaspora visible minority communities that their experience reflects God's own salvific journey of migrating from heaven to become human and take the form of a servant. From this identification and reflection of God's own marginality, diaspora communities can experience God's comfort in being one with them in their struggles even as he calls them to persevere and become agents of his message of salvation. Diaspora Visible minority Christian communities are missionaries of relational marginality. From these communities, God is calling for the formation of hermeneutical communities that will bring to light the truth and God's revelation in scripture.

Leading people into relational marginality requires, first of all, transformational leadership that is effectuated by the leader's relationship with the Triune God. Only in such relationship will a leader understand the nature of God's experience of migration and marginality as a salvific act. In this understanding, a person is then transformed as a new being. To be under Christ is to be liberated from the values of the world that seeks centrality and power. Instead, the new being is now subject to Christ where the only calling is to invite others into this relationship. Relational marginality is a state of being in relationship with Christ and under Christ's rule. It is to be subjected to a marginality that is liberative.

From this new position, the leader is not just concerned with the power structures of the world but is captive to the new calling to preach the good news of salvation. This does not denote that a diaspora leader is not concerned with the injustices and discrimination against visible minorities that forces immigrants to experience powerlessness and devaluing. This is still a calling for all Christians in the light of justice as essential to God's nature. It means that to

---

[381] Hill, "Just Power," 112.
[382] Hill, "Just Power," 112.

be in the new marginality is to experience genuine freedom in Christ that gives value and sense of equality to a person in the midst of dominance in this world. Thus, "there is neither Jew nor Gentile, neither slave nor free, nor is there male and female, for you are all one in Christ Jesus" (Gal. 3: 28).

Figure 8 shows the patterns and consequences of relationships between the Triune God, the host society, the diaspora visible minorities that lead to leadership development and empowerment of Christian diaspora leaders which impacts relationships through transformation into relational marginality. At the same time, the work of a leader is also working for justice for the diaspora communities and at the same time inviting unbelievers into a relationship with God. This will then lead to the transformation of society or the host culture.

Figure 7. Leading from Marginality to Relational Marginality

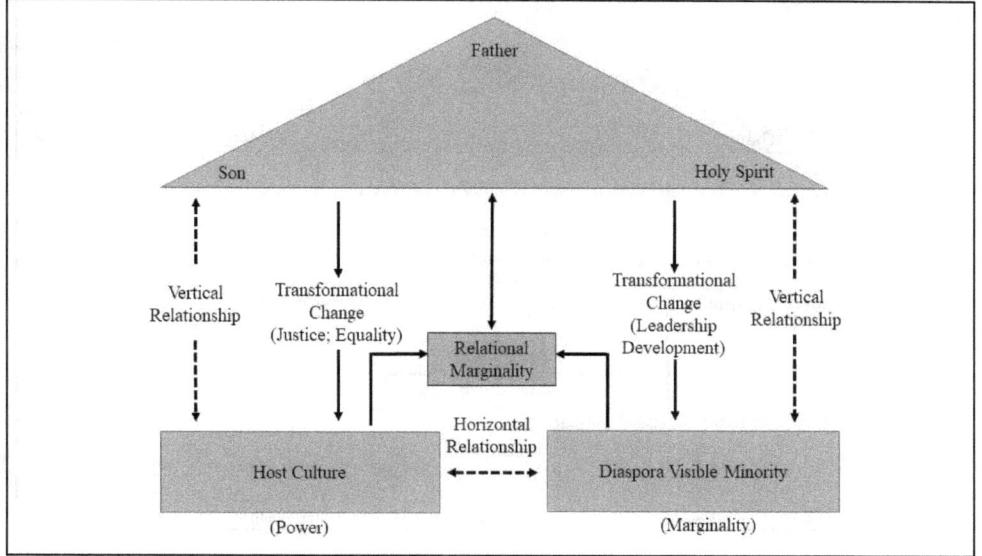

The relationship with the Triune God leads to transformational leadership which impacts the diaspora community to enter into this relationship and be in a state of relational marginality. As the leader continues to invite the host culture to the gospel, this ultimately leads to the transformation of culture. This model of transformation from marginality to relational marginality follows the three phases of transformational change—Being, Belonging, and Becoming.[383]

Being, as an individual phase, begins with the transformation of individuals from diaspora visible minority communities and of individuals in host societies through relationship with the Triune God. The transformation leads to the

---

[383] Wan and Raibley, *Transformational Change in Christian Ministry*, 11.

Belonging phase where there is formation of a hermeneutical community, and a horizontal relationship between the host society and diaspora community also develops into conditions of justice and equality. It then leads to the phase of Becoming where marginality is transformed into relational marginality and leadership development among Christian diaspora visible minorities leads to their transformation as agents of relational marginality. This will ultimately fulfill God's purpose of redeeming his humanity and bring them into the embrace of his Kingdom. It is a journey of being treated as strangers (*paroikos*) in a host society and become agents of God's Kingdom, his household (*oikos*). Figure 9 presents the transformational journey of diaspora visible minorities into the three phases of transformational change.

Figure 8. Phases of Transformational Change

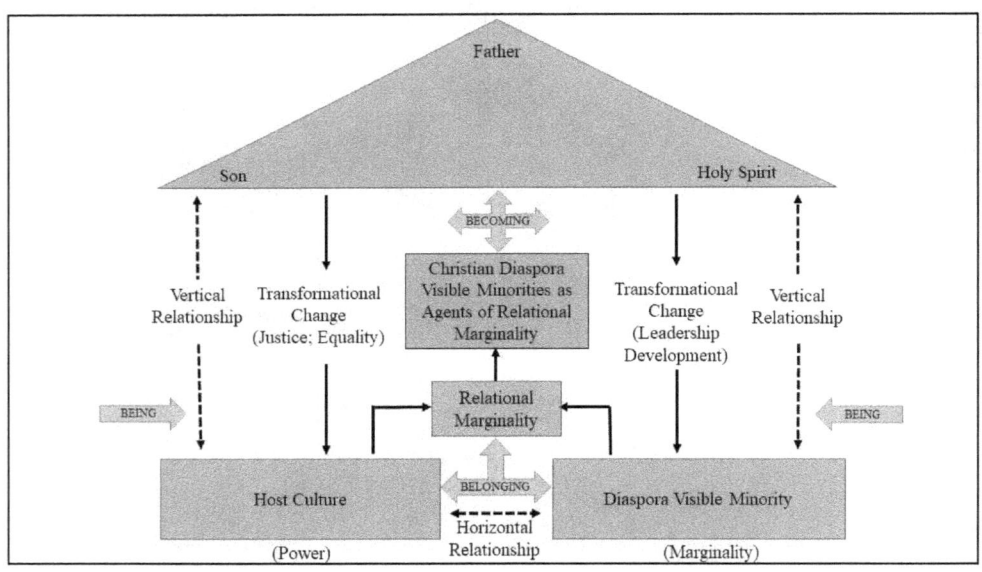

Summary

The condition of marginality needs to be understood from an integrative framework that considers not only the social or human dimension or causes of marginality but of the impact and consequences of transgressional change brought about by human rebellion against God and sinfulness. The relationship with the Triune God brings with it transformational changes in human relations that would lead to justice and equality. The relationship of diaspora visible minorities with the Triune God leads to changes in conception of their migration journey and marginality as central to God's redemptive work.

This missiology of marginality is transformative in leading diaspora people into spaces of leadership where their leadership is recognized, and where they are active in the act of mission within the societies and communities where they are situated.

CHAPTER 8

SUMMARY, CONCLUSIONS, AND RECOMMENDATIONS

Introduction

This book sought to understand the nature of marginality of diaspora visible minorities from interdisciplinary, biblical, scriptural, theological, and missiological perspectives. The key consideration of the study was exploring into the ethnicity of diaspora visible minorities as a factor in the experience and condition of marginality. It further investigated the composition of diaspora visible minorities in Canada and delved into research and literature underscoring these marginal experiences and conditions to contextualize the study. The research then proceeded to explain the missiological understanding of marginality through a relational framework that served as the basis for leadership development of Christian diaspora visible minorities.

Summary of Findings

Nature of the Ethnicity and Marginality of Diaspora Visible Minorities through Interdisciplinary, Biblical, Scriptural, Theological, and Missiological perspectives

The concept of marginality is understood differently from varied social science disciplines. In the field of Sociology, marginality has been originally understood in the context of immigrants where both Parks and Stonequist view this as a state of cultural ambivalence of people living in-between cultures. It was Weisberger, however, who categorically delineated it as a condition of cultural marginality of immigrants. Further study by Cullen and Pretes suggests that marginality is a condition of social exclusion. Marginality is understood as a social construct.

In Economics, marginality is seen as the condition of having limited or no access to resources. This understanding is closer to Marx's concept of alienation. Alienation is about an experience of being excluded from control over resources and production processes.

In the field of Psychology, there is also a strong tendency to connect this with the experience of immigrants where they experience alienation and loss. Thus, marginality is an experience of dissonance with the host culture and a feeling of inferiority.

Anthropology views marginality as anchored on the race, socio-economic status, and ethnic identities of people that define what their socio-cultural position is in a society that leads to discrimination and inequality. This position results in social stratification and limited access to resources. It is in the concepts of race and ethnicity that people are considered as "the other" in a host society.

An integrative view of marginality provides an understanding beyond human conditions but seeks to underscore the holistic perspective of reality as including Theo-culture and the impact of the spiritual realm on human existence or what Hiebert calls as the "excluded middle." Marginality is the product of transgressional change or humanity's rebellion and sin against God.

Biblical and Scriptural Perspectives of Migration and Marginality

The biblical and scriptural perspectives of migration and marginality reveal how God weaved both as central in his mission to reveal himself to the nations and redeem humanity. From Genesis to Revelation, biblical narratives speak of his purpose to scatter people as vehicle for his purpose. In this migration journey, God selected people (both the nation of Israel and individuals) to be his messengers. The calling for these messengers includes the experience of marginality, whether they are aliens in a foreign land, becoming slaves, or as ordinary people without any significant social status. In the New Testament, he intentionally migrated from heaven to earth through Christ and took on the form of a slave. Christ on the cross is the ultimate act of marginality to redeem humanity.

Scripturally, marginality is seen as a kingdom value as God calls his people not only to consider themselves as foreigners on this earth but to live as Christ lived who humbled himself. Through this experience and condition, he calls his people to show compassion and hospitality, show justice, and invite people in community.

Theological Perspective of Marginality

In both experience of migration and marginality, God expresses the message of his centrality. From a theological perspective, the call to marginality is a call to dependence and faith in God. It is a transformed marginality that is not a product of transgressional sin but of believer's relationship with him. In this experience of marginality, it is relational as it proceeds from one's relationship with the Triune God.

The experience and condition of marginality, particularly in the context of immigrants, does not connote acquiescence to injustice, discrimination, and social exclusion, but a call to stand up for the oppressed. While he calls his followers to forgo the quest for centrality, he calls them to pursue justice for those in the margins. As God is a God of justice, then he demands his people and all of creation to pursue justice. His modelling of marginality is to give voice to those in the margins.

Missiological Perspective of Ethnicity

Ethnicity is a significant factor in the marginality of diaspora visible minorities within Canada. Their ethnicity makes them distinct from western host societies who are mostly of Caucasian background. Thus, the experience of European immigrants is different from visible minorities. Ethnic marginality is not a new phenomenon as there are biblical stories of ethnic discrimination. Central to this is the conception of other ethnicities as foreigners and are considered as 'the other.' This explains God's commandment to love the strangers or foreigners and treat them as native born. There are significant biblical texts that call God's people to show justice and hospitality to foreigners in both the Old and the New Testament.

As ethnicity is tied to the experience of marginality of immigrants, such ethnicity is connected to God's intention for their migration in his plan for humanity, including his pluralistic purpose and his commandment for people to scatter. Missiologically, the scattering of people fits into his overall plan for redeeming the nations. This culminates in his ingathering of nations as reflected in the book of Revelation where the diversity of God's people is given front and center focus in the fulfillment of his kingdom.

From a theological perspective, ethnicity is an expression of God's Triune nature, his creative process, and an expression of his missionary character.

The Nature of Ethnicity and Marginality of Diaspora Visible Minorities in Canada

To ground the book on empirical foundations, the book looked into the ethnicity of diaspora visible minorities and their condition and experience of marginality. Gleaning from primary data, the research revealed that visible minorities in Canada are considered distinct from the Anglo-European majority due to their distinct features and culture which is the factor in their marginality.

Visible minorities consist mainly of South Asians, Chinese, Black, Filipino, Latin American, Arab, Southeast Asian, West Asian, Korean, and Japanese. The term visible minority is in itself a categorization of distinction and there is a pervading concern regarding the use of the term as it is in itself seen as a discriminatory term. Current conceptions tend to be geared to the use of the term "racialized people" as this denotes their experience of racism and discrimination. In this regard, this focuses on the nature of 'race' as a categorizing factor as it is a social construction designed in the 17th century by Caucasian Anthropologists to group people according to status in society with white people considered as having superior physical attributes while the rest are considered inferior. The term 'visible minority' was coined to highlight their inequitable treatment and provide them with equitable measures in Canadian society and government policies.

Canada has a unique social character due to the emphasis on immigration to fuel economic growth. Currently, one in five Canadians are foreign born. The largest number of migrants come from India, China, and the Philippines. This migration trend is gradually changing the population characteristics of the nation. This change is also changing church profiles with immigrant churches seen as filling in the pews of churches and is even changing the nature of evangelicalism towards a more conservative direction.

Research and studies clearly show, however, that diaspora visible minorities experience discrimination, exclusion, and marginalization. This is not a new phenomenon as there is historical trend in the treatment of diaspora visible minorities that includes their direct migration exclusion starting from the time that Chinese migrants were taken in as laborers for railway construction and later additional migrants were prevented from entering through the Chinese Exclusion Act in 1923. Other visible minorities experienced similar treatment such as South Asian immigrants who were prevented from leaving their docked ship due to fierce public opposition.

There has been measures to address systemic discrimination proffered by the Canadian government through the Multiculturalism Act and Employment Equity Act, but these do not fully address the ongoing racism and discrimination. In the area of education and labor market participation, visible minorities are put at a disadvantage with their academic and professional credentials not given equal value with that of European immigrants. Visible minorities are also experiencing lower labor force participation, particularly the Japanese, Chinese, Korean or Arab/West Asian communities. Generally, visible minorities have higher unemployment rate than non-racialized Canadians. Thus, there is the "racialization of poverty" in Canada due to lower income for visible minorities.

Health access is another area of marginality as health access is influenced by race or ethnicity. Studies prove that discrimination is one of the determinants of health. One study revealed that "in Canada, racialized, immigrant and refugee groups are most at risk for the negative health effects that result from persistent health disparities, arising from race, socio-economic status, poverty, citizenship status, and other social determinants, which expose them to macro-structural and micro-situational inequalities."[384]

Visible minorities also have lower social and political participation. This is manifested in lower representation in the House of Commons. A study revealed that "while the rates of civic participation of racialized Canadians are generally similar to the rest of the population, their representation in management

---

[384] Waldron, "The Impact of Inequality on Health in Canada."

positions is considerably lower, and their voter turnout and political engagement are somewhat lower compared with other Canadians."[385]

Missiological Understanding of Diaspora Marginality through a Relational Framework

Marginality of diaspora visible minorities, while a negative condition, is central to God's missiological purpose of redeeming the nations and is reflective of his redemptive act in Christ who migrated from heaven and took on the form of a servant and died on the cross to pay for humanity's sin. For Christian diaspora visible minorities, their experience and condition of marginality needs to be anchored on God's modeling. In understanding their experience as having redemptive significance, marginality must be viewed through the nature of God himself and his redemptive action. This is the concept of relational marginality.

There are already existing transformational models and understanding of marginality. Jung Young Lee coined the concept of new marginality where a Christian immigrant has to anchor his experience as a recognition of God's right to centrality and believers are positioned to be in dependence upon God. He sees Christ as the epitome of the new marginality where the core of his divine marginalization is his incarnation. As marginal persons, Christians are called to be in the world but not of the world.

Woosung Calvin Choi coined the term positive marginality to affirm the value of ethnic minorities not as victims or outsiders or always looking at themselves from the lens of social conflict but as contributing members of society. He defined positive marginality through five key concepts: embrace, engage, establish, embody, and exhibit.

From these transformative models, the book affirms the need for a scriptural and missiological understanding of marginality through the concept of Relational Marginality. Relational Marginality affirms the scriptural call to redirect negative human experience to a life-affirming one where God affirms his purpose for such experience for people on the move. The missiology of marginality stems from who God is—a relational Triune God who is in relationship with humanity, seeking to redeem humanity from sinfulness and transform them in his image. Marginality could only be providentially understood in the context of relationships. From his relationship with his creation (vertical), God calls his redeemed people to live out such redemption in a spirit of loving relationship to others (horizontal), even to those who are persecutorial towards believers (Matt. 5: 40-44; Lk. 6: 29). Relational marginality is not acquiescence to the experience of exclusion, discrimination, and injustice. Believers must work for a just world as God is a God of justice

---

[385] Statistics Canada, "Portrait of the Social, Political and Economic Participation of Racialized Groups."

who seeks to liberate his people from the clutches of unbridled use of power. Marginality is not just an issue of justice and a push to shift the dynamics of power relations to liberate immigrants from such a state but to understand the message of God and his desire for his creation through this experience. From this transformational and relational perspective, the condition of marginality provides an understanding that marginality is an agency for mission, a template for Christian living, and a call for Christian diaspora people to be agents of God's mission.

Relational Understanding of Marginality as Basis for Leadership Development

Christian diaspora visible minorities' leadership development is a must to lead church formation into its exilic identity and direct missional efforts towards relational marginality based on their lived experience. Their leadership development has to be anchored in key areas of leadership formation.

It is imperative that Christian diaspora communities need to anchor their experience on scriptural injunctions. As such, they need to form a hermeneutical community where their shared experience of marginality is reflected in the light of scripture. As God's redemptive act is relational in both vertical and horizontal dimensions, a clear understanding of marginality as having a redemptive purpose must also be done in a relational context or formation of a community. In understanding scripture together, diaspora peoples are also called to reflect on their experience of marginalization while simultaneously being called to be leaders and teachers in decentering humanity.

Diaspora visible minorities represent God's diversity in his kingdom. As they live out their Christian lives in a multicultural or multiethnic context, Christian diaspora communities could not continue having monocultural tendencies and monocultural gathering. A call to mission is a call to cross cultures. In this regard, Christian diaspora visible minorities could serve well as cultural mediators. This requires equipping in intercultural competency. Being an immigrant does not make one interculturally competent.

Lastly, the issue of power dynamics is the central theme that impacts the lives of diaspora visible minorities. It is this power issue that marginalized them in the first place. Stallard proposed that creating leadership space for immigrants require the formation of diverse leadership teams in mission and ministry in an urban context.[386] In this manner, it provides space for people from other ethnicities (visible minorities for this book) to be in leadership positions and recognize their giftings and skills in mission and ministry.

---

[386] Stallard, "The Development of Multicultural Teams in the Book of Acts."

Hill, however, goes further by proposing to address the power dynamics within the church and establish power sharing with ethnic minorities.[387] In reflecting on Acts 6, they created a solution where the marginalized group was empowered to solve their own problems that led to the emergence of leaders among them.[388]

Diaspora Visible minority Christian communities are missionaries of relational marginality. Their lived experience with marginality lets them identify with the salvific work of God in Christ.

Conclusion

The book provided a comprehensive survey of the nature of marginality of diaspora visible minorities starting from the analysis of the concept from the perspective of different social science disciplines and then defining it from an integrative framework. The biblical scriptural, theological, and missiological foundations of ethnicity and marginality provided key understanding of the redemptive purpose of the ethnicity and marginality of visible minorities. The survey of studies on the nature of marginality of visible minorities in Canada provided empirical basis of their lived experience. The use of relational framework provided a distinct understanding of marginality as an agency for God's mission. All these analyses served as bases in charting the leadership development requirement for Christian diaspora leaders.

The book concludes that the condition of marginality of diaspora visible minorities needs to be understood from an integrative framework that considers not only the social dimension or causes of marginality but on the broader understanding of reality that considers Hiebert's excluded middle and Wan's conception of reality that looks at the supracultural dimension of God's relationship with humanity. A key factor in this understanding of marginality is transgressional change brought about by human rebellion against God and sinfulness.

While marginality is a negative experience from a social dimension perspective, the integrative perspective enables for a transformative understanding when people are in positive relationship with the Triune God. The relationship with the Triune God brings with it transformational changes in human relations that would lead to justice and equality. The relationship of diaspora visible minorities with the Triune God leads to changes in conception of their migration journey and marginality as central to God's redemptive work.

The book concludes that utilizing Relational Interactionism as a framework in understanding human experiences and social realities bring an important ingredient in transforming perspectives towards a broader and integrative

---

[387] Hill, "Just Power."
[388] Hill, "Just Power," 112.

analysis of these realities as not purely adverse, but as conditions that are purposeful. Relational Interactionism points to a transformational dimension of the impact of transgressional change brought about by human sinfulness and by the powers of evil principalities. Relational Interactionism also points to the power of the Triune God who is the center of all things. His transformational power elevates human experience beyond social conflict and utilizes these experiences towards the fulfillment of his sovereign plan of redemption of his creation.

Relationship is the central characteristic of this transformation. Relationship is the key. God's relationship with humanity transforms their experience from positions of power dynamics and social conflicts into places of positive transformational change that uplifts their conditions to a state of calling. In this regard, the marginality of diaspora visible minorities is transformed into a new state of being where such state is reflective of God's own salvific act of redeeming the world through his marginality in Christ. The place of marginality is now a place of celebration for Christian diaspora communities.

While relational marginality is a movement from conceiving it as result of transgressional change to transformational change, it should not just be understood as a change from one condition to another or a change of one (negative) perspective towards a new (positive) perspective. It is rather a missional calling. Christian diaspora minority persons and communities are called to live out their transformed marginality as a vehicle for mission to the different nations represented by diaspora communities in Canada and the host society.

The transformation of marginality of diaspora visible minorities into a missional calling necessitates the importance of valuing and equipping Christian diaspora leaders into mission and church leadership. As Butcher, McGrath, Sibley-Bentley, and Wieland state: "where migrants themselves progress into key church and mission leadership roles they are very often able to assist in reducing attitudinal barriers for others."[389]

Recommendations

The book provided an exhaustive treatment of diaspora marginality and contributed to a new perspective on a transformed marginality. The study also revealed key areas of consideration for additional research and applications. Key recommendations are provided herein.

---

[389] Andrew Butcher et al., "Mission to and from Diaspora: Influencing the Context for Mission," (2016): 12, https://www.researchgate.net/publication/302557573_Mission_to_and_from_diaspora_influencing_the_context_for_mission.

Methodologically, there is a need to test the theoretical perspectives in the lived experience of diaspora visible minorities in Canada through primary research whether through a survey, ethnographic study, or phenomenological research. The latter could provide a qualitative study on the phenomenon of marginality that delves into the lived experience of different diaspora visible minority groups. As the book relied on archival research only, a process of triangulation could further substantiate deeper understanding of their marginality experience and highlight their lived experiences. Primary research could also shed light on areas that are not evident in secondary data analysis or review of literature. Case studies on marginality that provide exhaustive treatment of the condition of each visible minority group would be a meaningful research endeavor that could add further information on the extent and nature of marginality. Leadership development would be significantly bolstered by these primary data and could shape the content of any training curriculum. A research process that provides people the opportunity to speak is a step in giving them a voice and essential to the empowerment goal. Thus, a research process that has an emic perspective is central to biblical justice and affirms the value of people who are in the margins. Primary data collection through interviews would also provide nuances on the nature of marginality that could not be gleaned from secondary data analysis.

Thematically, there is a need to look into the nature of marginality of Christian diaspora leaders in the church and mission formation. One key area of concern that is not addressed by the book is how marginality is experienced and processed by Christian diaspora leaders to give them voice in mission and church leadership. Cursory observation would point to the reality that mission organizations and many multi-ethnic churches are still led by those in the majority culture. Another area of concern is the composition of the Board of Directors of these mission organizations. Representation is important and diaspora visible minority leaders need to have representation in leadership of mission organizations, major churches, and denominations.

Theoretically, it is imperative to do a comparative study of diaspora marginality by investigating marginality conditions in other Western countries. Migration is a global phenomenon, and this movement of people requires a global approach in addressing marginality. Determining leadership development models done by churches, mission organizations, and denominations for ethnic minorities and racialized groups could be avenues for replication by Canadian churches and mission organizations.

Theologically, it is recommended to further study the gathering purpose of God. There is substantial biblical and scriptural investigation of God's purpose for migration as central to his plan for scattering humanity in this book. As marginality is one of the consequences of the gathering of people groups in a host country, it is crucial to explore the theological foundation for multicultural church formation and how marginality is discussed in Bible studies, preaching, and other teaching platforms. The church formation in Antioch in the book of Acts is an important starting point for this theological exploration.

Missiologically, a missiological exploration of hosting and hospitality between settler communities and indigenous peoples is an important area of consideration. It was mentioned in the previous chapter that a study on indigenous relations could not be covered by this book. Would diaspora visible minorities have good standing in building relationships with the Indigenous communities owing to this shared experience of marginality? Would they be effective agents of the gospel based on this shared experience? While it is not appropriate to equate marginality of the two groups on the same level, this shared experience could be an avenue for relationship-building, leading to gospel transformation.

The gospel compels Christian diaspora visible minorities to embrace their marginality as a kingdom value. Hopefully, host churches and host communities will also be transformed and respond to the gospel call to embrace and celebrate diversity. Canada's multiculturalism posture and the increasing number of visible minorities should lead both host churches and diaspora churches to explore partnership in mission and intercultural church formation. It is the hope of the author of this book that the research findings would lead to other research areas in exploring the nature of existing models of ministry and mission partnerships, and direct other missiological studies that serve in bringing light to various ways that God's Kingdom is manifested in Canada.

APPENDIX 1

RESEARCH DESIGN AND METHODOLOGY

Methodological Design

This missiological study on the role of diaspora marginality in mission utilized archival research. The rationale for the use of archival research rather than primary data collection is that it best answered the research questions. Archival research is a type of methodology that adheres to secondary data analysis.[390] The main type of archival research that was used was review of literature by studying books, research, and pertinent documents relative to immigrants' marginality.

The study used the STARS approach developed by Wan for an integrative process in its organization. The STARS approach creates not only interdisciplinary coherence but "integrates biblical study, theology, anthropology, demographic, statistic, etc., in order to achieve a high degree of coherence or unity in research and for the practice of Christian mission."[391] It is instructive that the lack of integration will lead to disciplinary myopia.[392]

The explanation of the STARS approach in Table 1 shows how such approach helps in connecting different disciplines into an analytical and in-depth understanding of a phenomenon, relating this to the current context, and delineating its relevance through practical applications. The understanding of the phenomenon is then grounded on the overarching scriptural and theological foundations.

Further explanation of the criteria is provided herein:

1. Scripturally Sound- As evangelicals, Scripture is to be the basis and guide of Christian faith and practice. It is axiomatic for evangelical Protestants based on the conviction of "sola scriptura."
2. Theologically Supported- A base of pragmatism/expedience is insufficient; rather, sound theology is essential and required.
3. Analytically Coherent- Not to be self-contradictory; rather it should be both consistent and coherent.
4. Relevantly Contextual- Not to be out of place; rather, required to be fitting for the context.

---

[390] Vogt, Gardner, and Haefelle, *When to Use What Research Design*, 86.
[391] Wan, "Inter-Disciplinary and Integrative Missiological Research," 5.
[392] Wan, "Inter-Disciplinary and Integrative Missiological Research," 2.

5. Strategically Practical- It is good to have scriptural/theological support with coherent theory and cultural relevance, which may be strategically put into practice

The study ensured that the propositions are scripturally sound. It is instructive at this stage to differentiate between biblical and scriptural. Biblical narratives are not universal or prescriptive in nature and usually are context specific. Scriptural injunctions are, however, universal and are "binding for people at all times."[393]

Theologically sound principles were then proffered as to how the immigrants' experience and state of marginality reflect God's providential work to bring about his mission.

The study sought to attain analytical coherence through review and analysis of relevant research and theories and grounding the findings on scripture and sound theology.

The contextual nature of the study was through analysis of the state of marginality of visible minority diaspora communities.

Research Procedures and Techniques

The use of the archival research design, particularly using literature review and secondary data analysis followed a five-fold step that delineated a logical sequence of research on marginality and mission that first explored the scriptural foundations, theological foundations, and proceeded to contextualization, implications, and application.

The phase 1 on biblical and scriptural exploration included an analysis of the lives of biblical personages from both the Old and the New Testaments and explored their experiences of migration and marginality and how these shaped their missional calling. A significant focus was done on the life of Jesus, particularly on the nature of God's incarnation in Christ. References on the incarnation in the New Testament had significant bearing in this analysis.

The theological and missiological foundations on phase 2 relied on the biblical and scriptural explorations and analyzed the theological implications. As defined, theologizing is the act of developing a theological argument and treating from a theological point of view the issue of marginality in the context of the immigrants' experience as based on scripture.

Phase 3 analyzed social science literature and research pertaining to diaspora marginality in Canada, particularly focusing on visible minorities. Analysis of primary research provided salient findings on the state of marginality of this immigrant group and ground the research on relevant

---

[393] For further explanation, see, Wan, "Inter-Disciplinary and Integrative Missiological Research," 6–7.

primary findings. This included the history of discrimination in Canada to delineate the systemic nature of such discrimination of visible minorities.

Phase 4 determined a framework for mission work among diaspora communities. The missiological implication both tackled the role of marginality in God's mission as well as its relevance to the way missions should be done towards and by diaspora communities through the relational framework.

Phase 5 dealt with the practical application on leadership development by looking at relational paradigm in equipping Christian diaspora leaders in mission to diaspora and by diaspora communities.

The choice of archival research was based on the fact that it best serves in answering the research questions.

The archival research approach utilized in this book is literature review and secondary data analysis. Vogt, Gardner, and Haeffele, categorically delineated several archival methodologies as inclusive of reviews of research literature, research synthesis, meta-analysis, database archives, organizational records, textual studies of documents, and new media, including various Internet sources such as Web pages and blogs.[394] They further clarified that the value of review of literature points to "databases and other archival sources that could be used by the researcher."[395]

Collection of Data

The research approach used purely archival research, utilizing review of literature and secondary data analysis. In using scriptural exploration, relevant tools in textual analysis and Bible research tools including character analysis and exegesis were utilized.

Relevant statistical data and studies about diaspora visible minorities in Canada was investigated. Statistical data, particularly that of Statistics Canada was the primary tool in grounding the research on empirical information. Word study and Biblical-Theological analysis were used in grounding the research on Scripture. The primary tool in this area was the use of Biblical-Theological approach. The approach used by Andreas J. Kostenberger and Desmond Alexander[396] was helpful methodological tool in this respect.

---

[394] Vogt, Gardner, and Haefelle, *When to Use What Research Design*, 89.
[395] Vogt, Gardner, and Haefelle, *When to Use What Research Design*, 89.
[396] Andreas J. Kostenberger and T. Desmond Alexander, *Salvation to the Ends of the Earth: A Biblical Theology of Mission* (Downers Grove, Il.: Intervarsity Press, 2020), 1–5.

BIBLIOGRAPHY

American Anthropological Association. "AAA Statement on Race." https://www.americananthro.org/ConnectWithAAA/Content.aspx?ItemNumber=2583.

Anderson, Bernhard W. *From Creation to New Creation: Old Testament Perspectives*. Eugene, Oregon: WIPF and Stock Publishers, 2005.

Anglin, Deidre M., Sabrina Ereshefsky, Mallory J. Klaunig, Miranda A. Bridgwater, Tara A. Niendam, Lauren M. Ellman, Jordan DeVylder, et al. "From Womb to Neighborhood: A Racial Analysis of Social Determinants of Psychosis in the United States." *American Journal of Psychiatry* 178, no. 7 (July 2021): 599–610. https://doi.org/10.1176/appi.ajp.2020.20071091.

Angus Reid Institute. "Faith and Immigration: New Canadians Rely on Religious Communities for Material, Spiritual Support," July 9, 2018. http://angusreid.org/faith-canada-immigration/.

Ashford, Bruce, and Scott Bridger. "Missiological Method." In *Missiology: An Introduction to the Foundations, History, and Strategies of World Missions*, edited by John Mark Terry, 31–40. Nashville, TN: B & H Academic, 2015.

Barreto, Eric. *Ethnic Negotiations: The Function of Race and Ethnicity in Acts 16*. Tübingen: Mohr Siebeck, 2010.

Bauckham, Richard. *The Theology of the Book of Revelation*. Cambridge: Cambridge University Press, 1993.

Bell, Avril. "Being 'at Home' in the Nation: Hospitality and Sovereignty in Talk about Immigration." *Ethnicities* 10, no. 2 (May 27, 2010): 236–56. https://doi.org/10.1177/1468796810361653.

Benet-Martinez, Veronica, and Jana Haritatos. "Bicultural Identity Integration (BII): Components and Psychosocial Antecedents." *Journal of Personality* 73, no. 4 (August 2005): 1015–50. https://doi.org/10.1111/j.1467-6494.2005.00337.x.

Berger, Peter L., and Thomas Luckmann. *The Social Construction of Reality: A Treatise in the Sociology of Knowledge*. London: Penguin Books, 1966.

Berry, David. "Canadian Multiculturalism Act." *The Canadian Encyclopedia*, March 25, 2020. https://www.thecanadianencyclopedia.ca/en/article/canadian-multiculturalism-act.

Bhugra, Dinesh, and Matthew A Becker. "Migration, Cultural Bereavement and Cultural Identity." *World Psychiatry* 4, no. 1 (February 2005): 18–24.

Bible.org. "What Does 'Nation, Kindred, Tongue and People' in Rev. 14 Mean?," January 1, 2001. https://bible.org/question/what-does-%E2%80%9Cnation-kindred-tongue-and-people%E2%80%9D-rev-14-mean.

Billson, Janet M. "No Owner of Soil: The Concept of Marginality Revisited on Its Sixtieth Birthday." *International Review of Modern Sociology* 18 (Autumn 1988): 183–204.

Block, Sheila, and Grace-Edward Galabuzi. "Canada's Colour Coded Labour Market." *Canadian Centre for Policy Alternatives and The Wellesley Institute*, March 2011.

Booth, Alison, Andrew Leigh, and Elena Varganova. "Does Racial and Ethnic Discrimination Vary across Minority Groups? Evidence from a Field Experiment," *IZA Discussion Papers*, May 2010.

Brannen, Mary Yoko, Stacey R. Fitzsimmons, and Yih-teen Lee. "Marginals as Global Leaders: Why They Might Just Excel!" *The European Business Review*. https://www.academia.edu/2417702/Marginals_as_Global_Leaders_Why_they_might_just_excel_.

Britannica.com. "Race," n.d. https://www.britannica.com/topic/race-human/Scientific-classifications-of-race.

Bryce, Emma, and Stephanie Pappas. "What's the Difference between Race and Ethnicity?" *livescience.com*, November 3, 2022. https://www.livescience.com/difference-between-race-ethnicity.html.

Burton, Mark, and Carolyn Kagan. "Community Psychology: Why This Gap in Britain?" *Manchester Learning Disability Partnership and Manchester Metropolitan University*, n.d.

Bush, Luis. "The Meaning of Ethne in Matthew 28:19." https://www.missionfrontiers.org/issue/article/the-meaning-of-ethne-in-matthew-2819.

Butcher, Andrew, George Wieland, Terry Mcgrath, and Victoria Sibley. "Mission to and from Diaspora: Influencing the Context for Mission," 2016. https://www.researchgate.net/publication/302557573_Mission_to_and_from_diaspora_influencing_the_context_for_mission.

Cambridge Advanced Learner's Dictionary & Thesaurus. "Migration." https://dictionary.cambridge.org/dictionary/english/migration.

Campbell, William S. "Differentiation and Discrimination in Paul's Ethnic Discourse." *Transformation* 30, no. 3 (July 2013): 157–268.

Carrington, William J., and Enrica Detragiache. "How Extensive Is the Brain Drain?" *Finance and Development: A Quarterly Magazine of the IMF* 36, no. 2 (June 1999). https://www.imf.org/external/pubs/ft/fandd/1999/06/carringt.htm.

Chaturvedi, Vinayak. "A Critical Theory of Subalternity: Rethinking Class in Indian Historiography." *Left History: An Interdisciplinary Journal of Historical Inquiry and Debate* 12, no. 1 (Spring/Summer 2007): 9–28. https://doi.org/10.25071/1913-9632.15042.

Choi, Woosung Calvin. *Preaching to Multiethnic Congregation: Positive Marginality as a Homiletical Paradigm*. New York: Peter Lang Inc., International Academic Publishers, 2015.

Cornelissen, Louis. "Religiosity in Canada and Its Evolution from 1985 to 2019." *Statistics Canada*, October 28, 2021. https://www150.statcan.gc.ca/n1/pub/75-006-x/2021001/article/00010-eng.htm.

Cullen, Bradley T., and Michael Pretes. "The Meaning of Marginality: Interpretations and Perceptions in Social Science." *The Social Science Journal* 37, no. 2 (2000): 215–29.

Davis, Ken L. "Building a Biblical Theology of Ethnicity for Global Mission." *The Journal of Ministry & Theology*, Fall 2003, 91–126.

Deyoung, Kevin. "Theological Primer: Perichoresis." *The Gospel Coalition*, November 19, 2020. https://www.thegospelcoalition.org/blogs/kevin-deyoung/theological-primer-perichoresis/.

Dobson, Sarah. "Skilled Immigrants Overlooked for Leadership Roles." *TRIEC*, April 25, 2016. https://triec.ca/skilled-immigrants-overlooked-for-leadership-roles/.

Ellie, Massey Howes. "Durkheim's Anomie in a Time of Crisis," July 9, 2020. https://liberalarts.org.uk/durkheims-anomie-in-a-time-of-crisis/.

Elwell, Frank W. "Wallerstein's World-Systems Theory." http://www.faculty.rsu.edu/users/f/felwell/www/Theorists/Essays/Wallerstein1.htm.

Essex, Keith H. "The Abrahamic Covenant." *The Masters Seminary Journal* 10, no. 2 (Fall 1999): 191–212.

Flemming, Dean. *Contextualization in the New Testament: Patterns for Theology and Mission*. Downers Grove, Il.: AVP Academic, 2005.

Frideres, J.S. "Racism." *The Canadian Encyclopedia*, February 7, 2006. https://www.thecanadianencyclopedia.ca/en/article/racism.

Garris, Zachary. "Did God Intend for Israel to Have a King? (1 Samuel 8)." *Knowing Scripture*, March 5, 2019. https://knowingscripture.com/articles/did-god-intend-for-israel-to-have-a-king-1-samuel-8.

Gatto, Fr. Mark. "The Holy Trinity: A Vision of How Humanity Should Be," June 16, 2019. https://www.catherineofsienachurch.ca/the-holy-trinity-a-vision-of-how-humanity-should-live/.

Gatzweiler, Franz W., and Heike Baumüller. "Marginality—A Framework for Analyzing Causal Complexities of Poverty." In *Marginality:*

Addressing the Nexus of Poverty, Exclusion and Ecology, edited by Joachim von Braun and Franz W. Gatzweiler, 27–40. Dordrecht: Springer Netherlands, 2014. https://doi.org/10.1007/978-94-007-7061-4_2.

Gatzweiler, Franz W., Daniel Callo-Concha, Jan Henning Sommer, Janina Kleemann, and Manfred Denich. "Marginality from a Socio-Ecological Perspective." In *Marginality: Addressing the Nexus of Poverty, Exclusion and Ecology*, edited by Franz W. Gatzweiler and Joachim von Braun, 57–65. Dordrecht: Springer Netherlands, 2014. https://doi.org/10.1007/978-94-007-7061-4_2.

Gatzweiler, Franz W., Baumüller Heike, Christine Ladenburger, and Joachim von Braun. "Marginality: Addressing the Root Causes of Extreme Poverty." *ZEF Working Paper Series 77*. Center for Development Research, University of Bonn, 2011.

Gibson, Margaret A. "Immigrant Adaptation and Patterns of Acculturation." *Human Development* 44, no. 1 (2001): 19–23.

Gorospe, Athena. "Case Study: Overseas Filipino Workers." *Evangelical Review of Theology* 31, no. 4 (October 2007): 369–75.

Government of Canada. "Canadian Multiculturalism Act," July 1, 1988. https://laws-lois.justice.gc.ca/eng/acts/c-18.7/page-1.html.

Government of Canada. "Employment Equity Act," December 15, 1995. https://laws-lois.justice.gc.ca/eng/acts/E-5.401/page-1.html#h-215135.

Government of Canada. "Notice – Supplementary Information for the 2023-2025 Immigration Levels Plan." *Promotional Material, November 1, 2022*. https://www.canada.ca/en/immigration-refugees-citizenship/news/notices/supplementary-immigration-levels-2023-2025.html.

Government of Canada. "Significant Events in History of Canadians of Asian Heritage," April 29, 2021. https://www.canada.ca/en/canadian-heritage/campaigns/asian-heritage-month/important-events.html.

Government of Canada. "The Komagata Maru Incident of 1914." https://www.canada.ca/en/parks-canada/news/2016/08/the-komagata-maru-incident-of-1914.html.

Granger, Nathaniel. "Marginalization: The Pendulum Swings Both Ways." *Unbound*, April 5, 2013. https://www.saybrook.edu/unbound/marginalization/.

Grant, Tavia, and Denise Balkissoon. "'Visible Minority': Is It Time for Canada to Scrap the Term?" *The Globe and Mail*, February 6, 2019. https://www.theglobeandmail.com/canada/article-visible-minority-term-statscan/.

Hall, Jonathan. *Hellenicity: Between Ethnicity and Culture*. Chicago: University of Chicago Press, 2002.

Halwani, Sana. "Racial Inequality in Access to Health Care Services." *Ontario Human Rights Commission*, December 2004. https://www.ohrc.on.ca/en/race-policy-dialogue-papers/racial-inequality-access-health-care-services.

Hammer, Mitchell R. "The Intercultural Development Inventory: A New Frontier in Assessment and Development of Intercultural Competence." In *Student Learning Abroad*, edited by M. Vande Berg, R.M. Paige, and K.H. Lou, 115–36. Sterling, VA: Stylus Publishing, 2012.

Han, Jessie. "Institutional and Social Perspectives on Visible Minority Representation in Canadian Parliament." *Politicus Journal*, nd.

Hiebert, Paul. *Missiological Implications of Epistemological Shifts: Affirming Truth in a Modern/Postmodern World*. Harrisburg, PA: Trinity Press International, 1999.

Hiebert, Paul G. "The Flaw of the Excluded Middle." *Missiology: An International Review* X, no. 1 (January 1982): 35–37.

Hiebert, Paul G. *The Gospel in Human Contexts: Anthropological Explorations for Contemporary Missions*. Grand Rapids, Michigan: Baker Academics, 2009.

Hill, Daniel. "Just Power: Ten Principles for Building Intercultural Leadership Teams." In *Intercultural Ministry: Hope for a Changing World*, edited by Grace Ji-Sun Kim and Jann Aldredge-Clanton, 111–23. Valley Forge, PA: Judson Press, 2017.

Hook, Bell. *Feminist Theory: From Margin to Center*. Boston: South End Press, 1984.

Horowitz, Asher. "Max's Theory of Alienation." Lecture, Department of Political Science, Faculty of Liberal Arts and Professional Studies, York University, 2012 2011. https://www.yorku.ca/horowitz/courses/lectures/35_marx_alienation.html.

Hou, Feng, Grant Schellenberg, and John Berry. "Patterns and Determinants of Immigrants' Sense of Belonging to Canada and Their Source Country," October 18, 2016. https://www150.statcan.gc.ca/n1/pub/11f0019m/11f0019m2016383-eng.htm.

Howell M., Brian, and Jenell Paris W. *Introducing Cultural Anthropology: A Christian Perspective*. Michigan: Baker Academic, 2011.

Hudick, Katie. "Community Psychology's Impact on Public Health and the Experience of Marginalization." *Community Psychology*, n.d., 20.

Immigration, Refugees and Citizenship Canada. "2022 Annual Report to Parliament on Immigration," December 21, 2022.

https://www.canada.ca/en/immigration-refugees-citizenship/corporate/publications-manuals/annual-report-parliament-immigration-2022.html.

Jablonski, Nina G., and George Chaplin. "Human Skin Pigmentation as an Adaptation to UV Radiation." *Proceedings of the National Academy of Sciences* 107, no. supplement_2 (May 5, 2010): 8962–68. https://doi.org/10.1073/pnas.0914628107.

Jobling, David. "Sojourner." In *The New Interpreter's Dictionary of the Bible*, edited by Katharine Doob Sakenfeld, 5:314–16. Nashville, TN: Abingdon, 2009.

Kallen, Evelyn. *Ethnicity and Human Rights in Canada*. Third Edition. Ontario, Canada: Oxford University Press, 2003.

Kankesan, Tharsni. "Understanding Bicultural Identity and Its Impact on the Association between Discrimination and Well-Being," PhD Dissertation, University of Toronto, 2010.

Keller, Timothy. "The Bible and Race." *Life in the Gospel*, March 2020. https://quarterly.gospelinlife.com/the-bible-and-race/.

Kostenberger, Andreas J., and T. Desmond Alexander. *Salvation to the Ends of the Earth: A Biblical Theology of Mission*. Downers Grove, Il.: Intervarsity Press, 2020.

Kraus, Norman C. *The Authentic Witness: Credibility and Authority*. Grand Rapids: Eerdmans, 1979.

Kreitzer, Mark R. *The Concept of Ethnicity in the Bible: A Theological Analysis*. Lewiston, New York: The Edwin Mellen Press, 2008.

Lau, Sherman. "Is Multiculturalism 'Bad' for the Church?." *Mission Central*, October 4, 2019, https://www.missioncentral.ca/posts/2019/10/is-multiculturalism-bad-for-the-church.

Lau, Sherman. "The Influence of Canadian Multiculturalism on Ethnic Diversity in Evangelical Churches in Vancouver, British Columbia." DIS Dissertation, Western Seminary, 2022.

Lausanne Movement. "The Seoul Declaration on Diaspora Missiology." *Lausanne Movement*, November 14, 2009. https://www.lausanne.org/content/statement/the-seoul-declaration-on-diaspora-missiology.

Lebedev, Alexey Borisovich, Raviya Faritovna Stepanenko, German Nikolaevich Stepanenko, and Elena Vladislavovna Kuzmina. "Marginality in the Socio-Philosophical and Juridical Dimensions: The Experience of an Interdisciplinary Approach." *Revista San Gregorio*, no. 34 (November 2019): 6–13.

Lee, Jung Young. *Marginality: The Key to Multicultural Theology*. Minneapolis: Fortress Press, 1995.

Lee, Sang Hyun. "Pilgrimage and Home in the Wilderness of Marginality: Symbols and Context in Asian American Theology." In *Korean Americans and Their Religions : Pilgrims and Missionaries From a Different Shore*, edited by Ho Youn Kwon, Kwang Chung Kim, and Stephen R. Warner, 55–69. Pennsylvania: Pennsylvania State University Press, 2001.

Leeman, Jonathan. "Soteriological Mission: Focusing in on the Mission of Redemption." In *Four Views on the Church's Mission*, edited by Jason S. Sexton, 17–45. Grand Rapids, Michigan: Harper Collins Publishers, 2017.

Ma, Clayton. "Visible Minority." *The Canadian Encyclopedia*, May 5, 2021. https://www.thecanadianencyclopedia.ca/en/article/minorite-visible.

Mahalingam, Ramaswami. "Power, Social Marginality, and the Cultural Psychology of Identities at the Cultural Contact Zones." *Human Development* 51, no. 5–6 (2008): 368–73. https://doi.org/10.1159/000170898.

Maruskin, Joan. "The Bible as the Ultimate Immigration Handbook: Written by, for, and about Migrants, Immigrants, Refugees, and Asylum Seekers." *CWS Immigration and Refugee Program*, 2006.

Mathewson, Dave. "The Destiny of the Nations in Revelation 21:1-22:5: A Reconsideration." *Tyndale Bulletin* 53, no. 1 (2002): 121–42.

McAuliffe, Marie, Binod Khadria, and Céline Bauloz, eds. *World Migration Report 2020*. Geneva: IOM, 2019.

McRae, Matthew, and Steve McCullough. "The Story of Black Slavery in Canadian History." *Canadian Museum for Human Rights*, August 22, 2018. https://humanrights.ca/story/story-black-slavery-canadian-history.

Meister, Daniel, Erica Gagnon, Jan Raska, Lindsay Van Dyk, Monica MacDonald, Siniša Obradovic, and Steven Schwinghamer. "*Canadian Multiculturalism Policy*, 1971," n.d. https://pier21.ca/research/immigration-history/canadian-multiculturalism-policy-1971.

Meister, Daniel, Erica Gagnon, Jan Raska, Lindsay Van Dyk, Monica MacDonald, Siniša Obradovic, and Steven Schwinghamer. "The Chinese Immigration Act, 1885." *Canadian Museum of Immigration at Pier 21*, n.d. https://pier21.ca/research/immigration-history/the-chinese-immigration-act-1885.

Mezirow, Jack. "Learning to Think Like an Adult: Core Concepts of Transformative Theory." In *Learning as Transformation: Critical Perspectives on a Theory in Progress*, 3–33. San Francisco, CA: Josey-Bass, 2000.

Montagu, Ashley. *Man's Most Dangerous Myth: The Fallacy of Race*. 5th ed. London: Oxford University Press, 1974.

Moreau, A Scott, ed. *Evangelical Dictionary of World Missions*. Grand Rapids, Michigan: Baker Books, 2000.

Morin, Amy. "What's the Difference Between Race and Ethnicity?" *Verywell Mind*, October 19, 2022. https://www.verywellmind.com/difference-between-race-and-ethnicity-5074205.

Moyser, Melissa. "The Mental Health of Population Groups Designated as Visible Minorities in Canada During the COVID-19 Pandemic." *Statistics Canada*, September 2, 2020. https://www150.statcan.gc.ca/n1/pub/45-28-0001/2020001/article/00077-eng.htm.

Office of United Nations High Commissioner for Human Rights. "Racial Discrimination." *The United Nations*. https://www.ohchr.org/en/taxonomy/term/903.

Online Greek Word Study. "The Greek Word 'Glossa,'" March 29, 2016. https://www.bumchecks.com/biblecommentary/2016/03/29/the-greek-word-glossa/.

Ontario Human Rights Commission. "Racial Discrimination, Race and Racism (Fact Sheet)," n.d. https://www.ohrc.on.ca/en/racial-discrimination-race-and-racism-fact-sheet.

Oreopoulos, Philip. "Why Do Skilled Immigrants Struggle in the Labor Market? A Field Experiment with Thirteen Thousand Resumes." *American Economic Journal: Economic Policy* 3, no. 4 (2011): 148–71.

Ott, Craig, Stephen J. Strauss, and Timothy C. Tennent. *Encountering Theology of Mission: Biblical Foundations, Historical Developments, and Contemporary Issues*. Grand Rapids: Baker Academic, 2010.

Oxford Reference. "Diaspora." https://doi.org/10.1093/oi/authority.20110803095716263.

Palmer, Howard, and Leo Driedger. "Prejudice and Discrimination in Canada." *The Canadian Encyclopedia*, February 10, 2011. https://www.thecanadianencyclopedia.ca/en/article/prejudice-and-discrimination.

Park, Robert E. "Human Migration and the Marginal Man." *American Journal of Sociology* 33, no. 6 (1928): 881–93.

Perla, Armando. "The Canadian Charter of Rights and Freedoms." *Canadian Museum for Human Rights*, April 12, 2017. https://humanrights.ca/story/canadian-charter-rights-and-freedoms.

Pew Research Center. "Canada's Changing Religious Landscape." *Pew Research Center's Religion & Public Life Project*, June 27, 2013. https://www.pewforum.org/2013/06/27/canadas-changing-religious-landscape/.

Pierson E., Paul. *The Dynamics of Christian Mission: History Through a Missiological Perspective*. Pasadena, CA: WCIU Press, 2009.

Piper, John. "Slaves, Obey Your Masters; 1 Peter 2:18–20, Part 1." Desiring God, January 14, 2016. https://www.desiringgod.org/labs/slaves-obey-your-masters.

Pollock, Grace, Bruce Newbold, Ginette Lafrenière, and Sara Edge. "Perceptions of Discrimination in Health Services Experienced by Immigrant Minorities in Ontario." *Citizenship and Immigration Canada*, n.d.

Pratt, Geraldine. "From Registered Nurse to Registered Nanny: Discursive Geographies of Filipina Domestic Workers in Vancouver, B.C." *Economic Geography* 75, no. 3 (1999): 215–36. https://doi.org/10.2307/144575.

Precept Austin. "Philippians 2:11 Commentary," n.d. https://www.preceptaustin.org/philippians_211_commentary.

Quan, Hude, Andrew Fong, Carolyn De Coster, Jianli Wang, Richard Musto, Tom W. Noseworthy, and William A. Ghali. "Variation in Health Services Utilization Among Ethnic Populations." *Canadian Medical Association Journal* 174, no. 6 (March 14, 2006): 787–91. https://doi.org/10.1503/cmaj.050674.

Rawls, John. "Justice as Fairness: Political Not Metaphysical." *Philosophy & Public Affairs* 14, no. 3 (1985): 223–51.

Satzewich, Vic, and Nikolaos Liodakis. *"Race" and Ethnicity in Canada: A Critical Introduction*. Ontario, Canada: Oxford University Press, 2007.

Setzer, Claudia. "The Syrophoenician Woman." *Bible Odyssey*. https://www.bibleodyssey.org/people/related-articles/syrophoenician-woman.

Shepard, Jon. *Sociology*. 10th ed. California: Wadsworth Publishing Company, 2009.

Social Science LibreTexts. "Alienation," August 22, 2018. https://socialsci.libretexts.org/Bookshelves/Sociology/Introduction_to_Sociology/Book%3A_Sociology_(Boundless)/17%3A_Population_and_Urbanization/17.04%3A_Urban_Life/17.4F%3A_Alienation.

Sparknotes. "Karl Marx (1818–1883): Themes, Arguments, and Ideas." https://www.sparknotes.com/philosophy/marx/themes/.

Spencer, John R. "Sojourner." *Oxford Bibliographies*, June 26, 2019. https://www.oxfordbibliographies.com/view/document/obo-9780195393361/obo-9780195393361-0266.xml.

Stackhouse Jr., John G. "The Rise and Fall (and Rise?) Of Evangelicalism in Canada." *Evangelical Fellowship of Canada*, September 11, 2017. https://www.evangelicalfellowship.ca/Communications/Articles/September-2017/The-rise-and-fall-(and-rise-)-of-evangelicalism-in.

Stallard, Stephen Christian. "The Development of Multicultural Teams in the Book of Acts: A Model with Application to Urban North America." PhD Dissertation, Southeastern Baptist Theological Seminary, 2020.

Statistics Canada. "Generation Status: Canadian-Born Children of Immigrants." https://www12.statcan.gc.ca/nhs-enm/2011/as-sa/99-010-x/99-010-x2011003_2-eng.cfm.

Statistics Canada. "Immigrants Make up the Largest Share of the Population in over 150 Years and Continue to Shape Who We Are as Canadians," October 26, 2022. https://www150.statcan.gc.ca/n1/daily-quotidien/221026/dq221026a-eng.htm.

Statistics Canada. "Immigration and Ethnocultural Diversity: Key Results from the 2016 Census," October 25, 2017. https://www150.statcan.gc.ca/n1/daily-quotidien/171025/dq171025b-eng.htm?indid=14428-1&indgeo=0.

Statistics Canada. "Impacts of COVID-19 on Immigrants and People Designated as Visible Minorities," October 20, 2020. https://www150.statcan.gc.ca/n1/pub/11-631-x/2020004/s6-eng.htm.

Statistics Canada. "Participation Rates," November 30, 2015. https://www150.statcan.gc.ca/n1/pub/71-222-x/2008001/sectiona/a-participation-activite-eng.htm.

Statistics Canada. "Portrait of the Social, Political and Economic Participation of Racialized Groups," May 17, 2022. https://www150.statcan.gc.ca/n1/daily-quotidien/220517/dq220517c-eng.htm.

Statistics Canada. "The Canadian Census: A Rich Portrait of the Country's Religious and Ethnocultural Diversity," October 26, 2022. https://www150.statcan.gc.ca/n1/daily-quotidien/221026/dq221026b-eng.htm.

Statistics Canada. "Visible Minority of Person," December 2, 2015. https://www23.statcan.gc.ca/imdb/p3Var.pl?Function=DEC&Id=45152.

Stonequist, Everett V. *The Marginal Man: A Study in Personality and Culture Conflict*. New York: Charles Scribner's Sons, 1937.

Thoennes, Erik. "What Is Theology?" *The Good Book Blog - Talbot School of Theology Faculty Blog*, May 16, 2016. https://www.biola.edu/blogs/good-book-blog/2016/what-is-theology.

Thomas, Ren. "The Filipino Case: Insights into Choice and Resiliency among Immigrants in Toronto," 2011. https://renthomas.ca/wp-content/uploads/2009/11/The-Filipino-Case-Insights-into-choice-and-resiliency-among-immigrants-in-Toronto.pdf.

Thompson, Brenda. "An Overview of Old Testament Principles on Reaching the Refugees in Our Midst." *International Journal of Frontier Missions* 2, no. 4 (October 1985): 363–68.

Tira, Sadiri Joy, and Enoch Wan. "The Filipino Experience in Diaspora Missions: A Case Study of Christian Communities in Contemporary Contexts." *Evangelical Missiological Society*, April 5, 2008. http://www.wcc2006.info/fileadmin/files/edinburgh2010/files/Study_Process/EDINBURGH%20COMMISSION%20VII%20tira%20diaspora.pdf.

Tomchuk, Travis. "The Doctrine of Discovery." *Canadian Museum for Human Rights*, November 2, 2022. https://humanrights.ca/story/doctrine-discovery.

TOW Project. "Gleaning (Leviticus 19:9-10)." https://www.theologyofwork.org/old-testament/leviticus-and-work/holiness-leviticus-1727/gleaning-leviticus-19910.

Turner, Victor. "Liminality and Communitas." In *The Ritual Process: Structure and Anti-Structure*, 94–113, 125–30. Chicago: Aldine Publishing, 1969.

United Nations. "Committee on Elimination of Racial Discrimination Considers Report of Canada," February 23, 2012. https://www.ungeneva.org/en/news-media/press/taxonomy/term/175/45070/committee-elimination-racial-discrimination-considers.

United Nations. "International Convention on the Elimination of All Forms of Racial Discrimination," December 21, 1965. https://www.ohchr.org/en/instruments-mechanisms/instruments/international-convention-elimination-all-forms-racial.

United Nations. "Report of the Committee on the Elimination of Racial Discrimination, Seventy-First Session," August 30, 2007. https://www.un-ilibrary.org/content/books/9789210558549/read.

United Nations High Commissioner for Refugees. "Figures at a Glance." UNHCR, June 18, 2020. https://www.unhcr.org/figures-at-a-glance.html.

Vogt, W. Paul, Dianne C. Gardner, and Lynne M. Haefelle. *When to Use What Research Design*. New York: Guilford Press, 2012.

Waldron, Ingrid RG. "The Impact of Inequality on Health in Canada: A Multi-Dimensional Framework." *Diversity & Equality in Health and Care* 7, no. 4 (2010). https://diversityhealthcare.imedpub.com/abstract/the-impact-of-inequality-on-health-in-canada-a-multidimensional-framework-1943.html.

Wan, Enoch. "Narrative Framework for Relational Transformational Change," 2021.

Wan, Enoch. "Relational Transformational Leadership: An Asian Christian Perspective." *Asian Missions Advance*, April 2021, 2–7.

Wan, Enoch, and Mark Hedinger. "Transformative Ministry for the Majority World Context: Applying Relational Approaches." *Occasional Bulletin*, Spring 2018.

Wan, Enoch, and Jon Raibley. *Transformational Change in Christian Ministry*. 2nd Ed. Portland, OR: Western Academic Publishers, 2022.

Weisberger, Adam. "Marginality and Its Directions." *Sociological Forum* 7, no. 3 (1992): 425–46.

Wieland, George M. "Finding Communitas in Liminality: Invitations from the Margins in the New Testament and in Contemporary Mission." In *We Are Pilgrims: Mission From, In and With the Margins of Our Diverse World*, edited by Darren Cronshaw and Rosemary Dewerse, 71–82. Dandenong: UNOH, 2015. https://www.academia.edu/33650300/Finding_Communitas_in_Liminality_Invitations_from_the_Margins_in_the_New_Testament_and_in_Contemporary_Mission_1.

Wilson, Janelle. "Marginality: A Key Concept Revisited." *Psychology Today*, September 14, 2015. https://www.psychologytoday.com/ca/blog/stories-the-self/201509/marginality-key-concept-revisited.

Wolf, Miroslav. *Exclusion and Embrace: A Theological Exploration of Identity, Otherness, and Reconciliation*. Nashville, TN: Abingdon Press, 2019.

Wright, Christopher J.H. *The Mission of God: Unlocking the Bible's Grand Narrative*. Downers Grove, Illinois: IVP Academic, 2006.

Wu, Tony. "Bicultural Identity." In *Encyclopedia of Child Behavior and Development*, edited by Sam Goldstein and Jack A. Naglieri, 238–39. Boston, MA: Springer US, 2011. https://doi.org/10.1007/978-0-387-79061-9_331.

Xu, Xiao. "Immigrants Providing a Boost to Declining Church Attendance in Canada." *The Globe and Mail*, December 22, 2017. https://www.theglobeandmail.com/news/british-columbia/immigrants-providing-a-boost-to-declining-church-attendance-in-canada/article37423409/.

Zaman, Habiba. "Racialization and Marginalization of Immigrants: A New Wave of Xenophobia in Canada." *Labour/Le Travail* 66 (Fall 2010): 163–82.

www.ingramcontent.com/pod-product-compliance
Lightning Source LLC
Chambersburg PA
CBHW060322050426
42449CB00011B/2603